Key Stage 3
Developing Lit.

SENTENCE LEVEL

GRAMMAR ACTIVITIES FOR LITERACY LESSONS

year
9

Christine Moorcroft and Ray Barker

A & C BLACK

Contents

Standard English and language variation

Glossary

Acknowledgements

The authors and publishers are grateful for permission to reproduce the following:
p. 22 extract from *Blitzcat* by Robert Westall (Macmillan Children's Books, 1989); **p. 24** extract from *The Week*, 3 August 2002; **p. 28** extract from *Foods that Harm, Foods that Heal* (Reader's Digest, 1996) by permission of The Reader's Digest Association Limited; **p. 30** extract from *Stormchaser* by Paul Stewart and Chris Riddell (Corgi Books, 2000). Used by permission of The Random House Group Limited; **p. 34** extract from *Introducing Archaeology* by Magnus Magnusson (Bodley Head, 1972); **p. 37** extract from *The Week*, 20 July 2002; extract from *Great Sporting Mishaps* by Geoff Tibballs (Robson Books, 2001); **p. 38** extract from *The Scotsman*, 2 August 2002; **p. 39** extract from *Letts Study Guide Key Stage 3 Geography* by Mike Clinch (Letts, 1999); **p. 42** extract from *Collins Gem: Insects* by Michael Chinery (HarperCollins, 1999). Reprinted by permission of HarperCollins Publishers Ltd. © Michael Chinery, 1999; **p. 44** extract from *The Whole Story: A Walk Around the World* by Ffyona Campbell (Orion, 1996); **p. 46** extract from *How Weather Works: Understanding the Elements* by René Chaboud (Thames and Hudson, 1994); **p. 48** extract from *Basic Web Page Creation using Word 2000* by A. A. Richards (Payne Gallway, 2000); **p. 50** extract from *King of Shadows* by Susan Cooper (Bodley Head, 1999). Used by permission of The Random House Group Limited; **p. 52** extract from *One Hundred Ways for a Cat to Train its Human* by Celia Haddon (Hodder & Stoughton, 2001). Reproduced by permission of Hodder and Stoughton Limited; text adapted from *Collins Gem: Dogs* by Wendy Boorer (HarperCollins, 1999). Reprinted by permission of HarperCollins Publishers Ltd. © Wendy Boorer, 1999; **p. 60** extracts from the *Daily Mirror*, 29 November 1919.

Published 2003 by A & C Black Publishers Limited
37 Soho Square, London W1D 3QZ
www.acblack.com

ISBN 0-7136-6485-1

The authors and publishers would like to thank Claire Truman for her advice in producing this series of books.

A CIP catalogue record for this book is available from the British Library.

Printed in Great Britain by St Edmundsbury Press Ltd, Bury St Edmunds, Suffolk.

A & C Black uses paper produced with elemental chlorine-free pulp, harvested from managed sustainable forests.

Introduction

Key Stage 3 Developing Literacy: Sentence Level

Key Stage 3 Developing Literacy: Sentence Level is a series of photocopiable resources for Years 7, 8 and 9, designed to be used during English lessons or in other subjects across the curriculum to improve grammar and sentence construction. They are also ideal for homework. The books focus on the Sentence level strand of the Key Stage 3 National Strategy *Framework for teaching English: Years 7, 8 and 9*.

Each book supports the teaching of English by providing a series of activities that develop essential literacy grammar skills. Literacy, of course, includes more than these basic skills, but language is about communication, and grammar and punctuation are essential in creating meaning. Writers need to develop an awareness of the effects of grammar and punctuation so that they can use them effectively – leaving them free to concentrate on developing, arranging and constructing ideas.

Grammar involves more than analysing sentences and being able to identify different classes of word, or learning the rules of grammar and punctuation. **Sentence Level Year 9** develops the pupils' appreciation of the importance of grammar and punctuation in communicating their intended meaning to their audience, and helps them to use grammar and punctuation to control the meaning of what they write. The activities in this book help the pupils to:

- write complex sentences, using a range of punctuation effectively;
- group and link sentences in paragraphs in a way which is suitable for the text-type;
- recognise and use the stylistic conventions of the main non-fiction text-types;
- explore and use different degrees of formality appropriate to the audience and purpose;
- recognise the differences between standard and non-standard English and when it is appropriate for each to be used.

How to use this book

Each double-page spread in this book is based on a Year 9 Sentence level objective. The left-hand page is a **starter** activity, which may be an OHT for use with the whole class, or an activity for the pupils to work on in pairs or small groups. The right-hand page provides a **consolidation** activity to reinforce the main teaching objective, followed by an **extension** activity (**Now try this!**) to extend the pupils' learning.

Starter activities

Each starter activity is designed to be used as a short introduction to the consolidation activity that follows it. Evidence has shown that lessons which start with a sharp focus on a specific objective – for only ten to fifteen minutes – grab the pupils' attention and ensure that the whole class is clear about what to do and about the expected outcome of the lesson. The starter activities in this book address the objectives in a direct and explicit way. They involve both reading and writing, and encourage fast-paced learning and interaction. A range of teaching and learning styles are used – from independent to teacher supported – focusing on the following key teacher interactions:

- direction
- demonstration
- modelling
- scaffolding
- explanation
- questioning
- exploration
- investigation
- discussion
- reflection and evaluation.

The starter activities in this book also provide valuable opportunities to revise previous learning. New terms are introduced and other important terms are revised during the starter activity; these are highlighted by being boxed or set in bold type. All the highlighted terms are explained in the glossary on page 64, which can be photocopied for the pupils to file and use for reference.

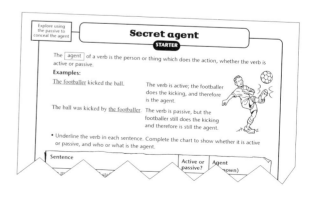

The starter activities can be photocopied and used in the following ways:

- as an OHT for whole-class teaching, with pupils giving answers orally or coming to the front to help complete the sheet;
- as a group activity, with each group working through the sheet or with different groups focusing on different parts of the sheet;
- as a timed activity, with the pupils completing as much of the sheet as possible within a time limit;
- in conjunction with appropriate class texts to help illustrate a principle;
- as preparatory work for an investigation, to be carried out for homework;
- as a stand-alone revision sheet for groups or individuals;
- as a tool for assessment.

Consolidation activities

The *Framework for teaching English: Years 7, 8 and 9* advocates that lessons should continue with a development of the main teaching points. The consolidation activities in this book can be used as the focus of this development, freeing teachers to work intensively with groups or individuals on the current objective.

The instructions in the activities are presented clearly to enable pupils to work independently. There are also opportunities for the pupils to work in pairs or groups, to encourage discussion and co-operation. Hints and reminders are given in boxes at the page margin.

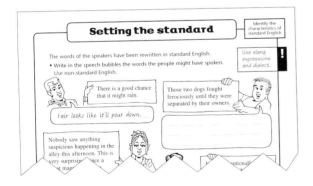

Extension activities

Each page ends with a **Now try this!** extension activity. These more challenging activities may be appropriate for only some of the pupils; it is not expected that the whole class should complete them. The pupils may need to record their answers in a notebook or on a separate piece of paper.

Organisation

The activities require very few resources besides dictionaries and, occasionally, examples of texts of different text-types: fictional and non-fictional recounts, reports (from booklets, leaflets and reference books), discussions and arguments (from newspapers, magazines or the Internet), and persuasive texts such as advertisements and charity or political leaflets. Examples of texts written in the first person will also be useful: for example, autobiographies, media interviews, diaries, letters, logbooks, memoirs, fictional narratives, eye-witness reports, poems, personal recounts and songs.

All the activities in this book are linked closely to the requirements of the *Framework for teaching English,* but it is not intended that they should be presented in any specific order, unless stated. This resource is versatile and is intended for teachers to use according to the literacy needs of their pupils.

Some of the activities can be linked with work in other subjects; however, it is envisaged that most of the activities will be carried out during English lessons.

Teachers' notes

The notes provided at the foot of the activity pages contain additional instructions for using the sheets. These can be masked before photocopying. The notes on pages 6–9 offer further practical advice on making the most of the activity sheets, including extra lesson ideas and suggestions for introducing the teaching objectives.

Useful websites

Websites which you may find useful include: www.educate.org.uk/teacher_zone/classroom/ literacy/sentence.htm (for lesson plans and interactive activities), http://geoffbarton.co.uk/ writing.htm (for teacher and pupil resources and articles on aspects of grammar), www.ccc. commnet.edu/grammar/ (for a guide to grammar and writing) and www.cool-reads.co.uk (which has book reviews by 10–15-year-olds).

The notes below expand upon those provided at the foot of each activity page. They give ideas for making the most of the activity sheets, including including suggestions for follow-up work and answers to selected activities.

Sentence construction and punctuation

Complex sentences (pages 10–11). This activity examines the structure of complex sentences. The **starter** activity revises main and subordinate clauses. The **consolidation** activity helps the pupils to recognise how subordinate clauses add information or ideas to sentences. In the **extension** activity (**Now try this!**) they combine simple sentences in a way which makes some of them main clauses and others subordinate clauses within complex sentences.

Sentence strategies (pages 12–13). In this activity the pupils consider the impact of different sentence structures. The **starter** activity presents a series of sentences which are written using different strategies. The **consolidation** activity encourages the pupils to choose sentence structures for their effect. As a follow-up, the pupils could look in texts they are studying for examples of sentences with similar structures to those in the starter activity; they could also look for other strategies to use as models.

Add to it (pages 14–15). This activity looks at ways of combining phrases and clauses into complex sentences. In the **starter** activity, there are several ways in which the pupils could construct the sentences (they could add more than one phrase or clause to each sentence). In the **consolidation** activity they are asked to use phrases and clauses to add information or ideas to simple sentences. The **extension** activity encourages them to edit a piece of their own work.

Punctuation power (pages 16–17). This activity concentrates on dashes and brackets. The pupils should be familiar with all forms of punctuation before they begin. The following examples will be useful for introducing the **starter** activity: (1) *Today, throughout the country – in hotels, bed-and-breakfast accommodation †and more than two million homes – people wake up to a cup of tea made by an automatic tea-making machine.* (2) *Edward VII heard about the new vacuum cleaners which had been invented, and ordered two – one for* Buckingham Palace and one for Windsor Castle. (3) *He told her that it was ten past eight (she already knew that) and proceeded to complain that she was ten minutes late.* (4) *The jumper was in her favourite colour (red) but it was too expensive.* The **consolidation** and **extension** activities ask the pupils to use dashes or brackets to add information to sentences.

Active to passive (pages 18–19). This activity looks at the way in which the use of active or passive verbs can affect the level of formality of a text. For the **starter** activity, it may be useful to discuss what is meant by 'active' and 'passive', using an example such as *The girl fed the cat. The girl* is the subject of the verb as well as being the agent (doing the action). The verb is active because the agent is the subject. In the sentence *The cat was fed by the girl, the girl* is still the agent of the verb (doing the action), but the verb is passive and the agent is not the subject of the verb. The **consolidation** and **extension** activities give more practice in using the passive voice and recognising contexts in which it is appropriate.

Secret agent (pages 20–21). This activity reinforces when it is appropriate to use the passive voice. The **starter** activity helps the pupils to identify active and passive forms, and the agent of verbs. They should realise on completing the **consolidation** activity that the passive form is more formal than the active and that the style of language which is required affects the writer's choice of verb form. As a follow-up, the pupils could collect examples of sentences containing passive verbs from various sources (such as notices, signs and leaflets), and explain why the passive has been used. They could try converting active sentences to passive and passive to active if this is possible (and, if it is not, explaining why).

Time for talk (pages 22–23). Use this activity to revise the punctuation and layout of dialogue. The dialogue in the **starter** activity does not follow all the conventions the pupils have learned: words such as *asked, replied* and *said* are omitted in places. In the **consolidation** activity the pupils write rules for the punctuation and layout of dialogue. They should refer to (and add to) their rules when writing dialogue in future. In the **extension** activity they compare the effects of dialogue and reported speech. This helps to emphasise that through grammar they can control the meaning of what they write.

Quote it (pages 24–25). In this activity the pupils investigate different uses of quotation marks. The **starter** activity provides a text containing quotations from people and from other texts. For quotations from other texts the full stop can follow the quotation marks because the quoted words are integrated into the sentence. The **consolidation** activity asks the pupils to write a short newspaper report. They should check their punctuation, especially at the ends of quotations and sentences. The **extension** activity asks them to write a text of the same genre, this time without prompts.

Way out sentences (pages 26–27). This activity focuses on unconventional sentence structures. The passage in the **starter** activity, by Charles Dickens, contains many 'non-sentences' which have no verb (for example, *A man of fact and calculations*) or no main clause (for example, *A man who proceeds upon the principle that two and two are four...*). Other sentences with interesting structures include *To his matter of fact home, which was called Stone Lodge, Mr Gradgrind directed his steps* (which delays introducing the subject of the sentence). The **consolidation** activity develops the pupils' understanding of what constitutes a sentence and helps them to recognise when it is effective to break the rules. In the **extension** activity they are invited to model their own writing on that of Dickens.

Paragraphing and cohesion

Plan it (pages 28–29). This activity focuses on the content of paragraphs. As the pupils undertake the **starter** activity, they should become aware of the main point of each paragraph (expressed in the opening sentence) and the ways in which this point is developed in the rest of the paragraph. The answers are: 1(e), 2(a), 3(c), 4(b), 5(d). The **consolidation** activity helps the pupils to write a paragraph to support its main point. You could model an example by thinking aloud about the planning of a paragraph: for example, 'I am going to discuss why cyclists are more likely to be injured than car drivers. I shall explain, with examples, that car drivers are protected by the car itself while cyclists have only limited protection. To introduce ideas I could use words and phrases such as: *Consider, Imagine that, What if* and *The main danger is.*'

Opening words (pages 30–31). In this activity the pupils consider the effect of opening sentences of paragraphs. The opening sentences in the **starter** activity prepare the reader for the rest of the paragraph: for example, the first one introduces the storms over Twilight Woods and leads the reader to expect further details about the storms and the woods. The **consolidation** activity encourages the pupils to apply what they have learned to a retelling of *The Emperor's New Clothes* (even if the pupils do not know the story, they should be able to work out what the opening sentences should be about). Their sentences can be short and to the point: for example, (1) *There was once an emperor who was very fond of fine clothes.* (2) *People came to the palace from far and wide to look at the emperor's clothes.*

A new development (pages 32–33). This activity looks at ways of developing paragraphs. The **starter** activity presents some points made at the beginning of different paragraphs from an argument. The pupils are asked to develop one of the paragraphs using their choice of connective words from the list. In the **consolidation** and **extension** activities, the pupils develop paragraphs for another argument.

Paragraph links (pages 34–35). This activity and those on pages 36–41 focus on connective words and phrases. The **starter** activity looks at the ways in which a writer can draw readers into the text and make them want to read on, by leaving out pieces of information at first and by adding detail bit by bit. The first paragraph (which is the first paragraph of the book) intrigues readers, inviting them to read on, through a 'mystery'. The **consolidation** activity asks the pupils to write their own paragraph. There is no reason why they should not copy some of the introductory and opening sentences of the starter passage, changing the words to match the object they have brought in; they can learn by modelling their writing on that of an experienced writer.

Pronoun purposes (pages 36–37). The **starter** activity focuses on the use of pronouns as connectives. Pronouns are used in the place of nouns. They are useful connectives in that they can refer back to ideas already mentioned as well as preparing for those to come. Personal pronouns are *I, me, you, he, him, she, her, it, we, us, they, them.* Possessive pronouns are *my, mine, your, yours, his, her, hers, its, our, ours, their, theirs.* Reflexive pronouns are *myself, yourself, himself, herself, itself, ourselves, yourselves, themselves.* Other types of pronouns which might need to be introduced include the following (it is not necessary for the pupils to learn the names of the different types): reciprocal pronouns (*each other, one another*), demonstrative pronouns (*Where did you find that?, These belong to me*), indefinite pronouns (*anybody, anyone, anything, everybody, everyone, everything, nobody, no one, nothing, somebody, someone, something*), interrogative pronouns

(*What...? Which...? Who...? Whom...? Whose...?*), relative pronouns (*the house that Jack built, the path which leads up the hill, the man who lives next door, the woman whom I visited, the girl whose dog was lost*) and distributive pronouns (*all, both, each, either, neither*). The **consolidation** activity asks the pupils to identify the pronouns in two passages and to consider the ways in which they are used. Draw out the use of pronouns as connectives (they refer back to people, things, places or ideas already mentioned).

Get connected (pages 38–39). The passage in the **starter** activity contains mainly connectives which link ideas according to a time sequence: for example, *afterwards, next, then*. The simple linking connectives *and* and *but* are used to join ideas, and pronouns (*where* and *who*) are used as connectives to refer back to people, places and things. The connective *so* links ideas in a way which suggests a reason or explanation. The non-chronological report in the **consolidation** activity uses a range of different types of connectives for different purposes. In the **extension** activity, the pupils consider which types of connectives are most likely to be used by particular text-types.

Locate the linkers (pages 40–41). The **starter** activity introduces connectives which refer back to earlier ideas or information in a text. The pupils are asked to underline the connectives they identify in the passage (a recount in the first person). Examples from the first paragraph include (in chronological order): *that, which, but, for, and, besides that, and, that, but, for, before, the first time, and, it, but, which, only, for, and that, that vault, but, who, that, and that, there, it, for over forty years, since, who, but, that, and*. Another passage from the same text is provided in the **consolidation** activity, with some of the connectives removed and supplied on a notepad. In order to find their correct places in the passage, the pupils are required to think about the meaning and purpose of each connective and the meaning it gives to the sentence.

Stylistic conventions of non-fiction

A matter of fact (pages 42–43). This activity helps the pupils to recognise the stylistic features of information texts. The **starter** activity provides a passage from an information book about insects. The stylistic conventions are: setting the broad category (introducing the topic in a general way, by saying how an insect can be distinguished from other similar animals); narrowing it down to be more specific (describing each section of the insect's body in detail); describing different aspects of the subject (giving some individual differences between insects); describing generic types (describing generic body parts such as the coxa, femur, tibia and tarsus). Other features include: verbs in the present tense (*have, are used, is*); connective words and phrases signalling distinctive categories of information (*such as, which, the latter, when present*); the third person (*an adult insect can, most insects have*); technical vocabulary with some description (*the pronotum is a tough plate..., a prominent rounded or triangular plate called the scutellum...*). In another lesson, the pupils could compile a glossary for the passage (with the help of a scientific dictionary). The **consolidation** activity invites the pupils to apply what they have learned to their writing; it also gives an example of how to make notes from a passage.

What's the story? (pages 44–45). This activity focuses on recounts. The **starter** activity provides an example of an autobiographical recount, whose stylistic conventions are: informal language style (simple vocabulary, slang and dialect expressions, contractions); mainly the first person, but also the third person; past tense; mainly the active voice (with the passive used where the agent is not important or is not specified); mainly time connectives; the use of dialogue or quotations; mainly simple punctuation (commas and full stops), although occasionally semi-colons and colons are used; and a range of simple, compound and complex sentences. In the **consolidation** activity, the pupils are invited to write another autobiographical recount based on notes from a biography. Those who undertake the **extension** activity will need to research a famous person; this could be linked with work in history or RE.

Explain yourself! (pages 46–47). The **starter** activity provides examples of the stylistic conventions of explanation texts: a formal language style (sophisticated vocabulary, no contractions or dialect terms, and indirect language, which does not address the reader directly); technical vocabulary; the third person; the present tense; mainly the active voice (with the passive used where the agent is not important or is not specified); nouns which do not refer to any specific item (*clouds, air*); connectives which indicate cause and effect (*because, in fact*); and mainly complex sentences (statements and some questions to add interest). The **consolidation** activity invites the pupils to apply what they have learned to their writing. Those who undertake the **extension** activity will need to research another aspect of weather; this could be linked with work in geography or science.

Step by step (pages 48–49). The **starter** activity uses an ICT text to revise the stylistic conventions of instructions. These include: a fairly informal and direct language style (addressing the reader directly as *you*); technical vocabulary (*home page, Web, scroll*); imperative verbs; the present tense; simple punctuation (full stops and commas); short, mainly simple sentences; 'signposts' to help the reader follow the text (arrows in this case, but bullets or numbers could also be used); a signal for the end of the process and a closing statement to help the reader evaluate what has been done (*Now you are ready to use your home page*). The **consolidation** activity presents a recount of a process (sending an email) and asks the pupils to convert it to instructions, using the starter passage as a guide.

Adapted (pages 50–51). In this activity the pupils investigate how stylistic and grammatical conventions can be adapted for effect. The passage in the **starter** activity comes from a fictional recount with narrative and dialogue. Instead of using the past tense throughout, the tense occasionally changes to the present (*Run round the big echoing space... try to catch someone*); this makes the action seem more real, as if the narrator were re-living it. Quotation marks are used, but words such as *said* are omitted, and sometimes it is difficult to tell who is speaking. This is intentional; the writer wants to create a feeling of chaotic action. This effect is intensified by the use of 'non-sentences' with no verb or no main clause. The **consolidation** activity asks the pupils to rewrite the passage from the starter activity, 'correcting' the grammar. This helps them to appreciate the effects of the grammatical adaptations used by the writer. Pupils who undertake the **extension** activity develop their understanding by comparing their changed version of the passage with the original. The 'correct' grammar, especially the use of words such as *said* to introduce speech, can sound stilted and slows down the action of the passage.

Language challenge (pages 52–53). This activity enables the pupils to compare the language styles of different text-types. The **starter** activity provides examples of the following text-types: (1) a first-person recount, (2) instructions, (3) an information text and (4) an argument. The **consolidation** activity asks the pupils to make a formal analysis of language styles, based on the discussion of the starter activity. In addition to person, tense, voice and connectives, they should consider the level of formality: an informal text is likely to use short simple or compound sentences, simple vocabulary, contractions, first and second person pronouns and dialect and slang terms.

Standard English and language variation

Setting the standard (pages 54–55) and **Write standard English** (pages 56–57). These activities concentrate on recognising non-standard forms of English and developing an appreciation of when standard and non-standard English are appropriate. The **starter** activities look at different forms of non-standard English, including slang and dialect expressions and text-message abbreviations. Text-message English is a form of jargon: other forms of jargon used by small groups of people include specialised ICT terms, scientific words, and words associated with interests such as chess. The **consolidation** and **extension** activities reinforce the pupils' awareness of common non-standard English forms, as well as developing their ability to write standard English. As a follow-up, they could rewrite the speech on page 56 as a newspaper report.

Small talk (pages 58–59). This activity investigates the differences between spoken and written language. The passage in the **starter** activity shows how intonation, body language and response to other speakers are lost when a conversation is transcribed, which can make it difficult to follow. The **consolidation** activity focuses on more specific language differences and the **extension** activity provides an opportunity for the pupils to carry out their own investigation.

Sign of the times (pages 60–61). This activity looks at changes in the English language between 1919 and the present day. The language of the passages in the **starter** activity might amuse the pupils because it sounds old-fashioned; they are asked to identify what produces this effect. The **consolidation** activity asks them to find words, expressions and sentence constructions which have entered the English language since 1919.

Foreign affairs (pages 62–63). This can be linked with word-level work on synonyms and word derivations. Possible answers to the **starter** activity include: *rise, mount, **ascend**; ask, **question**, interrogate; fast, firm, **secure**; kingly, **royal**, regal; holy, **sacred**, consecrated; fire, flame, conflagration; twist, **turn**, revolve; gum, **glue**, adhere; silly, **stupid**, injudicious; buy, **purchase/procure**, obtain; middle, centre, **nucleus**; call/yell, **cry**, exclaim; boldness, **bravery/courage**, fortitude; old, aged, **ancient**; heavy, massive, **substantial**; felon, criminal, reprobate; **temper**, fury, ire; end, **finish**, terminate; begin, commence, **initiate**.* The **consolidation** activity involves the brainstorming of synonyms and research into their derivations.

Complex sentences
STARTER

- Read the passage.
- Underline the | main clauses | in red.
- Underline the | subordinate clauses | in blue.

Remember, a main clause makes sense as a sentence on its own. **!**

Long ago, before anyone had thought of fertility treatment but when the spells cast by fairies and elves were just as effective, a king and queen sat in their palace and lamented the fact that they had no children.

In desperation they arranged a consultation with the top fairy of the land, who said that all would be well and that the queen would be pregnant before the end of the year.

Sure enough the queen gave birth to a daughter, who was welcomed with great celebrations, including a party to which all the fairies in the kingdom were invited – well, nearly all.

There was one fairy whom everyone had stopped inviting to their parties, mainly because she was such a bore that most of the guests would go home, leaving the party somewhat depleted.

The boring fairy decided that an image change was in order. This time she would get her own back by gatecrashing the palace party armed with a set of evil spells which she would cast on the hapless baby.

The king and queen soon guessed she must be around when they found eighty per cent of their guests yawning and the other twenty per cent putting on their cloaks.

A palace security guard, who should have done his job properly by keeping her out, found the intruder bending over the baby's cradle, muttering foul words under her breath – and issuing foul breath over the baby.

Teachers' note Split the class into groups and give each group a copy of this page. First revise main clauses and subordinate clauses (see page 64) and remind the pupils that a sentence should still make sense if the subordinate clauses are removed. Commas are often used to demarcate subordinate clauses. Also discuss the difference between simple and complex sentences. Allow five minutes for the pupils to underline the clauses, then invite feedback. Compare the responses of each group and ask how they identified the main and subordinate clauses.

Developing Literacy
Sentence Level
Year 9
© A & C BLACK

Complex sentences

• List the key facts or ideas communicated by the following | complex sentences |.

Write in note form. **!**

Complex sentences

1. The security guard raised the alarm, at which the king and queen and all the remaining guests who were still awake came rushing into the nursery.

2. They gasped when they heard the so-called boring fairy's voice rising to a crescendo: 'She will cut her finger on a spindle (or possibly a hand-drill, if she chooses non-gender-biased pursuits), and will bleed to death.'

3. The guests stopped yawning and the fairy stalked out, cackling, leaving the king shaking his fist and declaring that all spindles and hand-drills were to be removed from the palace that day.

4. The jaws of the palace servants dropped almost to their ankles as they realised that they would lose their day off after the party to track down and remove every spindle and hand-drill in the palace.

5. One of them piped up that there was no need to panic because he had heard a similar story in which the spell had been diluted by another fairy, who changed the death threat to a long sleep.

Key facts

– security guard raised alarm

NOW TRY THIS!

• Combine these simple sentences to make complex sentences.

You will need to change the order of the information and ideas. **!**

They would want to marry his daughter. He knew the story, too. He didn't want princes flocking to his palace from all over the world. They would cut their way through his garden. The king was having none of that nonsense.

They took them to the local tip. They hired horses and carts. The next day the palace servants set to work. They piled them high with spindles and hand-drills.

The good fairies would be invited but not the boring fairy. On her eighteenth birthday it was time for another party. The palace guards were to be extra vigilant. They were to keep her out. If they did not they faced the sack. The princess was kept safe.

Teachers' note As the pupils identify the key facts or ideas, they should become aware of how they are arranged in clauses within each sentence. During the plenary session, discuss the use of main and subordinate clauses in the sentences.

Sentence strategies

STARTER

- Write sentences using the following strategies. Use the completed sentence as a model to help you.

Strategy: Start a sentence with the *-ed* form of a verb.

Amazed, they watched open-mouthed as the aliens came out of the spacecraft.

Amused, she _____

Petrified, _____

Strategy: Start a sentence with the *-ing* form of a verb.

Reading the instructions, she could see where she had gone wrong.

Lifting his head, he _____

Leaving the house, _____

Strategy: Start a sentence with a conjunction .

Before she could open the door, she had to shovel away the snow.

Although there were no strawberries, _____

Because _____

Strategy: Start a sentence with a connective .

Meanwhile, three sheep found their way into the kitchen.

As a result, they _____

Afterwards _____

Strategy: Put the subject in a place other than the beginning of the sentence.

In the quiet of the morning, listening to the birds in the garden, she could forget that she lived in a city.

Through the window, _____

Finding nobody in, _____

During lunch, _____

Developing Literacy
Sentence Level
Year 9
© A & C BLACK

Sentence strategies

- For each notepad, try three different ways of structuring a sentence to communicate the ideas and information.
- Decide which of the three sentences is the most effective. Tick it.

Notepad 1:
- scared child
- old house
- night
- sees 'faces' in the shadows

Notepad 2:
- boy running through woods
- others chasing
- hides; hopes they won't find him

Notepad 3:
- advert
- most effective vacuum cleaner company produces
- must be tried to be believed

Notepad 4:
- something lurking in the corner of the shed
- wondering what it is

NOW TRY THIS!

- Take the most effective sentence from each set and split it into two or more sentences. Use different structures, for example:
  - a statement
  - a question
  - an exclamation
  - an imperative.

Teachers' note Encourage the pupils to use the sentence strategies they learned in the starter activity. They should decide (perhaps with a partner) what effect they want to create and then try different ways of writing the same information or ideas. See also the activity on pages 26–27.

Add to it

STARTER

- Cut out the cards.
- Combine | simple sentences | , | phrases | and | clauses | to make longer sentences.

Simple sentences

It was an enormous car.

Sean was wearing a strange jacket.

I'll be back by ten o'clock.

You could phone Yasmin.

A new leisure centre is going to be opened.

The girls opened the box.

I don't believe in magic.

There is no way out.

There were two small badgers.

Write your sentences.

Phrases

in the corner of the garden	*of the large maze*
with the jewelled lid	*with three rows of seats*
with green stripes and yellow spots	*beside the park*
if possible	*and tinted windows*
of any kind	*in the grounds of the castle*

Clauses

whose owner had never been seen	wondering what was inside
and we were embarrassed to be with him	if you remember
trying to hide	while there is time
as far as I can see	but I do not think it's necessary
and I never shall	Amy told me that

Teachers' note Split the class into groups and give each group a copy of this page. First discuss the meanings of 'simple sentence', 'phrase' and 'clause' (see page 64). Allow five minutes for the pupils to construct their sentences and encourage them to try combining the simple sentences, phrases and clauses in different ways. Invite feedback from the groups. You could challenge them to make the longest sentence they can and to punctuate it carefully to ensure that it makes sense.

Developing Literacy
Sentence Level
Year 9
© A & C BLACK

Add to it

- Rewrite these sentences, adding **phrases** and **clauses** to give extra information. Use **connectives** and punctuation to make the meanings of your sentences clear.

Use the questions to help you.

!

They followed the trail.

_____

_____

Where? Why? What was it like?

No one could see what was happening.

_____

_____

Where? Why couldn't they see?

You too could be a winner.

_____

_____

What could you win? How?

It is a disgrace.

_____

_____

What is a disgrace? Why?

As little as £2 could make a difference.

_____

_____

To what or whom could it make a difference? How?

There used to be twelve cinemas in the town.

_____

_____

When? How have things changed? Why?

NOW TRY THIS!

- Choose a piece of your own writing to edit.
- Look for sentences which can be improved. Rewrite them.

You could try:
- ☆ adding information in phrases or clauses
- ☆ using different connectives or punctuation
- ☆ combining or splitting sentences.

Teachers' note Revise the use of connectives before beginning the activity. Point out that sentence grammar such as connectives and punctuation can help the pupils to control the meaning of what they write. In the extension activity, encourage them to look for ways of combining ideas or information from different sentences. They should compare their edited work with the original.

Developing Literacy
Sentence Level
Year 9
© A & C BLACK **15**

Punctuation power
STARTER

You can use dashes to isolate – or add – an extra point within a sentence.

- Put dashes in the correct places in these sentences.

Instant coffee coffee beans made into a powder was invented by the Swiss company Nestlé.

Teflon is slippery more slippery than ice sliding on ice.

Amy scored a goal in her first game for United the goal which took the team to the semi-final.

The car was well ahead of its time with safety features such as seat belts and airbags items which were new to most people in those days.

Forrest E Mars brought to Britain a recipe for a new type of chocolate the Mars Bar with a layer of caramel and a layer of nougat, covered with milk chocolate.

You can use brackets to surround words (or groups of words) which are not the main part of the sentence, but added as an 'aside'.

- Put brackets in the correct places in these sentences.

Fry the onions, add the potatoes coarsely shredded and cook for another twenty minutes.

The prizes were presented by Rose Bloom the proprietor of the nearby Bloom's garden centre and a local councillor who is a keen supporter of local gardening enterprises.

They brought six horses two of them thoroughbreds and four Shetland ponies.

Salim was looking forward to moving to his new house a semi-detached cottage in Ayrshire but would miss his friends in Manchester.

They were wondering they had been wondering all week whether to have the old car repaired or to buy a new one.

Teachers' note Photocopy this page onto an OHT. Before asking the pupils to insert the dashes, read aloud the examples provided on page 6 and ask them to listen carefully for where the dashes should be placed. Write the sentences on the board. Invite a pupil to read out the first sentence on the OHT and ask one of the others to punctuate it. Discuss the meaning. Continue for the other sentences. Repeat this for brackets, again using the examples on page 6. Discuss the ways in which dashes and brackets are used and identify any sentences where either would be appropriate.

Developing Literacy
Sentence Level
Year 9
© A & C BLACK

Punctuation power

- Use dashes or brackets to add the information in the speech bubbles to the sentences. Rewrite the sentences.

1. The story goes that nylon was named after the cities New York and London.

invented by Wallace Carothers

2. When Trevor Bayliss worked on the design for his radio he worked in a shed in his garden.

a clockwork one

3. What was special about the baby buggy when it was first invented was its light weight and its clever folding mechanism.

only three kilograms

4. Cut the cake into three layers, then spread jam on the bottom layer and butter icing on the middle layer.

see the recipes for fillings

5. The first product ever to be logged using a bar code made history at exactly 8.01 a.m. on 26 June 1974.

a packet of chewing gum sold at a supermarket in Troy, Ohio

NOW TRY THIS!

- Rewrite these sentences. Use dashes or brackets to add information.

He lived in London for six years. It was difficult to tell who was speaking the truth.

They found a collection of old newspapers under the floorboards.

You could see the spire of the cathedral in the distance.

Crossing the road was extremely difficult. Her cats no longer killed birds.

Teachers' note Help the pupils to decide whether dashes or brackets would be better for separating the extra information from the main part of each sentence. During the plenary session, remind them that words contained within dashes or brackets are not the main part of the sentence and could be omitted without affecting its sense.

Developing Literacy
Sentence Level
Year 9
© A & C BLACK 17

Active to passive
STARTER

1. Wear tennis shoes on the courts.

2. Don't wear coloured T-shirts.

3. Put your valuables in a locker.

4. Don't bring animals onto club premises.

5. Please pay your subscription by 30 April.

6. You can sign in one guest per day.

7. If others are waiting, please limit your game to three sets.

8. Put the net away if you're the last to use the court.

9. Please make sure the clubhouse is locked if you're the last to leave.

10. Please leave quietly so you don't disturb local residents.

• Rewrite the tennis club rules in a more formal way. Use passive verbs.

HIGHFIELD TENNIS CLUB • CLUB RULES

1. Tennis shoes must be worn on the courts.

Teachers' note Photocopy this page onto an OHT. First revise active and passive verbs (see page 6). Explain how the verb in the first example has been changed: it was originally in the imperative (command) form and to make it passive, the auxiliary verb *be* has been added and *wear* has been changed to *worn*. The pupils should take turns to read aloud a rule and express it formally, using passive verbs. Encourage them to begin each rule in a different way: for example, *Members are required to..., It is suggested that...* Discuss whether the agent of the verb is the subject of each sentence.

Developing Literacy
Sentence Level
Year 9
© A & C BLACK

Active to passive

• Rewrite the space station rules in a more formal way. Use **passive** verbs.

1. Exercise during your designated exercise times.
2. Sleep in your designated sleep times.
3. Always start your shift on time.
4. No perfumed items.
5. No food other than space programme issue.
6. No pets.
7. Always get up when alarm clock sounds.
8. Never miss duty.
9. Take turns to clean the station.
10. Keep shower cubicle sealed when in use.
11. Clamp all loose equipment.
12. Check monitors every ten minutes.
13. Don't use space phone for personal calls.
14. No mobile space phones.
15. No spitting.
16. Keep your personal things in your locker.
17. Close all doors.
18. Don't open the exit hatch except for official procedures.

Space station rules

1. Crew members are required to exercise during designated exercise times.

NOW TRY THIS!

• List ideas for a report about an area which has been vandalised, spoiled by litter or suffers from a general lack of care.

• Write two versions of the report:
   (a) as an email to a friend
   (b) as a letter to your local council.

Decide whether active or passive verbs are appropriate.

!

Teachers' note The pupils should notice that, as well as altering the verb forms from the active to the passive, they change them from the imperative (command) form to the declarative (statement) form. For the extension activity, they will need to consider the level of formality of the two reports they are asked to write, and which verb forms will be appropriate for each.

Secret agent

STARTER

The | agent | of a verb is the person or thing which does the action, whether the verb is **active** or **passive**.

Examples:

The footballer kicked the ball.

The verb is active; the footballer does the kicking, and therefore is the agent.

The ball was kicked by the footballer.

The verb is passive, but the footballer still does the kicking and therefore is still the agent.

- Underline the verb in each sentence. Complete the chart to show whether it is active or passive, and who or what is the agent.

Sentence	Active or passive?	Agent (if known)
The management and staff welcome you to the Queen's Head Hotel.		
During your stay you have the choice of our two fine restaurants.		
High-quality informal meals are served in the Carvery.		
For a more formal meal we recommend the Red Rose restaurant.		
Our chefs use only the finest ingredients.		
Both restaurants are known for their range of fish dishes.		
Fish is freshly caught each day by local fishermen.		
We buy all our vegetables from local markets.		
The meat is produced by organic farms.		
A local butcher prepares every joint of meat.		
The meat is delivered daily.		
We serve various British and Continental cheeses.		
We have won several awards for our desserts.		
Our speciality is sticky toffee pudding.		
Our milk, cream and ice cream come from small local producers.		
Coffee is freshly ground for each serving.		
The lounge has oak beams and a log fire.		

Teachers' note Photocopy this page onto an OHT. Check that the pupils understand the difference between the agent, the subject and the object of a verb. The agent of an active verb is its subject: for example, *The girl drew a picture; The hotel has a swimming pool*. The agent of a passive verb (if it has one) is its object: for example, *The picture was drawn by the girl*. Invite the pupils to read the sentences aloud and to contribute to the completion of the chart. Discuss why passive verbs are used in many of the examples (usually because the action, rather than the agent, is important).

Developing Literacy
Sentence Level
Year 9
© A & C BLACK

Secret agent

If the **agent** of a verb is not important, it is often a good idea to use the **passive** form of the verb.

- Use the information in the speech bubbles to help you write a leisure club information leaflet. Use passive verbs.

1. We employ only qualified lifeguards and fitness instructors.

2. Instructors and lifeguards staff the gym and pool at all times.

3. Someone gives all new members a fitness test and gym instruction course.

4. We encourage members to seek advice from the instructors.

5. We advise users of the gym to warm up before exercising.

6. We have displayed clear instructions for the use of all equipment.

7. Members can hire equipment for most activities from the reception desk.

8. We ask members to pay a refundable deposit when hiring equipment.

About your leisure club

1. Only qualified lifeguards and fitness instructors are employed.

- Write a short information leaflet about your school. Use active or passive verbs as appropriate.

Teachers' note When the pupils have completed the consolidation activity, encourage them to read both versions of the sentences and to decide with a partner which is better in each case and why. Point out that in most texts a mixture of active and passive verbs is used; it is not necessary to use only one or the other.

Developing Literacy
Sentence Level
Year 9
© A & C BLACK **21**

Time for talk
STARTER

- Read the passage.
- Underline the spoken words using coloured pens. Use a different colour for each speaker.

Now the sky was full of the sound of returning aircraft. They no longer flew in any kind of formation; the faster overtook the slower in their rush for the coast. There were propellers spinning slowly in the slipstream. One Heinkel seemed to have no nose left; another lacked a wingtip.

'They've had a rare bashin',' said Sergeant Smith. 'And they never made London – never had the time. And they won't come back in a hurry.'

'You keep on saying they won't come back,' said Mrs Smiley, waspishly.

'The RAF means business, now.'

The next thing they saw seemed to prove his words, in a way that was beyond belief. Two Dorniers, flying higher than the rest, huddled close together, as if for mutual protection. And a Hurricane after them, a burning Hurricane, trailing oily smoke. The Hurricane slowly overtook them, but it didn't fire its guns. It simply gained, till it sat directly above them. Then it sat down on them, hitting them with blows of its wings, like a hen settling on eggs.

The three planes fell apart in ruin, tumbling over and over down the sky, like shot grouse. Just one parachute opened, as the wreckage fell burning behind the next hill.

'That was the Hurricane pilot,' said Sergeant Smith. 'He was ready to bail out; he had his cockpit-canopy open.'

'Shall we go and see… if he's all right?'

'We'd never find him – he's miles away by this time. Plenty of locals to see to him.'

'I hope so.' She felt he was very hard-hearted.

No more planes came. There was a sort of aching weariness in the air over the hill.

'Hey, look at that!'

Beneath them, unnoticed before, sat a rabbit. Up on its hind legs, ears upright, eyes staring. They watched for a long time; it did not move.

'Paralysed wi' fear,' said Sergeant Smith. 'Fancy rabbit pie for supper?' He got up, and moved towards it stealthily. Even when he got within a yard of it, it still didn't move.

'No,' shouted Mrs Smiley. Normally, a rabbit would be more than welcome. But she had seen too many deaths this afternoon.

From Blitzcat by Robert Westall

Teachers' note Ask the pupils to work in pairs and give each pair a copy of this page. They should notice that sometimes the spoken words are not preceded or followed by words such as *Mrs Smiley said* or *said Mrs Smiley*, but that in these cases it is obvious from the rest of the dialogue who is speaking. Ask the pupils to comment on the effect of these omissions. You could also discuss the way in which the writer uses dialogue to communicate character. Encourage the pupils to say what they have learned from the dialogue about the two characters.

Developing Literacy
Sentence Level
Year 9
© A & C BLACK

Time for talk

- Re-read the passage which contains the dialogue between Sergeant Smith and Mrs Smiley. Write some rules for punctuating speech and setting out dialogue.

Using speech marks Rule: _____ _____	Example: _____
Using a comma at the end of speech Rule: _____ _____	Example: _____
Using an exclamation mark at the end of speech Rule: _____ _____	Example: _____
Using a question mark at the end of speech Rule: _____ _____	Example: _____
Using a full stop at the end of speech Rule: _____ _____	Example: _____
Punctuating words that show who is speaking Rule: _____ _____	Example: _____
Setting out dialogue to show when a new speaker starts talking Rule: _____	Example: _____

NOW TRY THIS!

- Rewrite the passage without using speech marks.
- Compare the effect with the original.

Turn the spoken words into reported speech.

!

Teachers' note The pupils will need to refer to the passage in the starter activity. First revise what speech marks are for, and how a writer knows where to place them. During the plenary session, discuss which punctuation marks can be used at the end of spoken words, and their position in relation to the speech marks.

Quote it

STARTER

- Read the passage.
- Explain why quotation marks are used in each instance.
- Explain why double quotation marks are used in some places and single ones
  in others.

Leo McKern 1920–2002

Leo McKern, who has died aged 82, was one of
the "soundest and widest-ranging actors in Britain",
said Adam Benedick in the *Independent*. He excelled
in classical roles, and was a regular West End lead
in British and European drama. But to the wider
public, he was best known as Horace Rumpole,
"the ageing, grumpy, henpecked and endearingly
down-at-heel barrister in John Mortimer's TV series
Rumpole of the Bailey". Although he regretted
being typecast, McKern had great affection for
his alter ego. "With Rumpole," he once said,
"one comes to be reconciled to the fact that it
isn't half a bad thing to be stuck with."

McKern "was generous always in calling me the 'only begetter' of Rumpole,"
said John Mortimer in the *Daily Mail*, "but the character was born as a
partnership in which the actor had just as much to play as the writer." McKern
was perfect in the role: he had a "gruff voice which, touchingly, could be as
sweet as honey". And although short, and rather fat, he was dextrous and as
light on his feet as a dancer. On set, he told jokes, recited rude limericks and
could "roll a hat up his sleeve until it fell magically on his head". He was,
"quite simply, the only Rumpole". But for all their similarities – not least a
liking for claret – McKern was not Rumpole, said Adam Benedick. For one
thing, he lacked the barrister's "philosophical patience" and "steadiness of
purpose". "I'm not as loyal as Rumpers," he once observed. "I would have left
She Who Must Be Obeyed years ago."

Born in Sydney in 1920, McKern left school at 15 to work in a refrigerator
factory, only to lose his eye in an industrial accident. Later, he used his
disability to great advantage, adjusting the glass eye to any direction to give his
countenance a "peculiar and sometimes teasing ambiguity".

From Obituary of Leo McKern, *The Week*

Teachers' note Photocopy this page onto an OHT. Read the passage with the pupils and help them
to identify the places where quotation marks indicate speech and where they indicate quotations
from other sources (such as texts). Point out the use of single quotation marks within double ones
where there are quotations within speech. Also note the positioning of quotation marks before full
stops where the quotations are from other sources rather than passages of speech.

Developing Literacy
Sentence Level
Year 9
© A & C BLACK

Quote it

- Read the spoken words and information about a toddlers' paddling pool at a leisure centre.
- Write a newspaper report about the problems of keeping the pool open. Use quotation marks to indicate [direct speech] or quotations. You can also use [indirect speech] (reported speech) for variety.

Children can drown in water as shallow as five centimetres.

Safety guidelines

We usually look after much deeper water. It seems odd to have two lifeguards for a paddling pool only seven centimetres deep.

Steve Robinson, lifeguard

The paddling pool must be emptied and refilled every day.

Government regulations

The pool is costing taxpayers around £8,000 per year. It seems a rather draconian approach but we must comply with government regulations.

Raj Singh, local councillor

Pru Dent, parent

If the pool is not properly supervised, children could knock their heads and drown.

It seems ridiculous. Wouldn't most taxpayers rather see the money being spent more efficiently?

Ann Brooke, local councillor

Amberford council wonders if it is worthwhile keeping its toddlers' paddling pool open.

_____

_____

_____

_____

_____

_____

NOW TRY THIS!

- Write a short report about an event or controversial issue in your locality. Use quotation marks to indicate direct speech. Include references to other sources.

Teachers' note Revise direct and indirect speech. You could provide examples of newspaper articles containing quotations from people and written sources, for the pupils to refer to. Remind them that where the quotations do not represent direct speech, the full stop at the end of the sentence is placed after the speech marks.

Developing Literacy
Sentence Level
Year 9
© A & C BLACK **25**

Way out sentences

STARTER

- Read the passage.
- Underline any 'sentences' (ending with a full stop, exclamation mark or question mark) which are not, in fact, sentences.
- Underline any sentences which have an interesting structure.

Thomas Gradgrind, sir. A man of realities. A man of fact and calculations. A man who proceeds upon the principle that two and two are four, and nothing over, and who is not to be talked into allowing for anything over. Thomas Gradgrind, sir – peremptorily Thomas – Thomas Gradgrind. With a rule and a pair of scales, and the multiplication table always in his pocket, sir, ready to weigh and measure any parcel of human nature, and tell you exactly what it comes to. It is a mere question of figures, a case of simple arithmetic. You might hope to get some other nonsensical belief into the head of George Gradgrind, or Augustus Gradgrind, or John Gradgrind, or Joseph Gradgrind (all supposititious, non-existent persons), but into the head of Thomas Gradgrind – no, sir!

In such terms Mr Gradgrind always mentally introduced himself, whether to his private circle of acquaintance, or to the public in general. In such terms, no doubt, substituting the words 'boys and girls', for 'sir', Thomas Gradgrind now presented Thomas Gradgrind to the little pitchers before him, who were to be filled so full of facts.

To his matter of fact home, which was called Stone Lodge, Mr Gradgrind directed his steps. He had virtually retired from the wholesale hardware trade before he built Stone Lodge, and was now looking about for a suitable opportunity of making an arithmetical figure in Parliament. Stone Lodge was situated on a moor within a mile or two of a great town – called Coketown in the present faithful guide-book.

A very regular feature on the face of the country, Stone Lodge was. Not the least disguise toned down or shaded off that uncompromising fact in the landscape. A great square house, with a heavy portico darkening the principal windows, as its master's heavy brows overshadowed his eyes. A calculated, cast up, balanced, and proved house. Six windows on this side of the door, six on that side; a total of twelve in this wing, a total of twelve in the other wing: four-and-twenty carried over to the back wings. A lawn and garden and an infant avenue, all ruled straight like a botanical account-book. Gas and ventilation, drainage and water-service, all of the primest quality. Iron clamps and girders, fireproof from top to bottom; mechanical lifts for the housemaids, with all their brushes and brooms; everything that heart could desire.

Everything? Well, I suppose so. The little Gradgrinds had cabinets in various departments of science too. They had a little conchological cabinet, and a little metallurgical cabinet, and a little mineralogical cabinet; and the specimens were all arranged and labelled, and the bits of stone and ore looked as though they might have been broken from the parent substances by those tremendously hard instruments their own names; and, to paraphrase the idle legend of Peter Piper, who had never found his way into their nursery, If the greedy little Gradgrinds grasped at more than this, what was it for good gracious goodness sake, that the greedy little Gradgrinds grasped at!

From *Hard Times* by Charles Dickens

Teachers' note Ask the pupils to work in pairs and give each pair a copy of this page: to help low attainers, put them into mixed-ability pairs. Suggest that they use two different colours to distinguish between 'non-sentences' and those which have an interesting structure. Discuss why Dickens has used these unconventional sentence structures, and their effect in creating the character of Mr Gradgrind. The pupils should notice that the 'non-sentences' have the effect of creating a list of points about Mr Gradgrind and his house. See also the activity on pages 12–13.

Developing Literacy
Sentence Level
Year 9
© A & C BLACK

Way out sentences

- Re-read the passage about Mr Gradgrind. Write the 'non-sentences' on the chart and explain why they are not sentences.

> Look for the verbs. Look for the subjects of the verbs.

'Non-sentence'	Why it is not a sentence
Thomas Gradgrind, sir.	There is no verb

NOW TRY THIS!

- Write another paragraph in the style of the passage.

> It could be about a meal in Mr Gradgrind's house, or his clothes or the contents of his kitchen.

!

Teachers' note The pupils will need to refer to their completed copies of the starter activity. In the extension activity, the pupils should vary the structure of their sentences to create the effect they want. They should also use 'non-sentences' modelled on those of Dickens.

Plan it
STARTER

- Cut out the cards.
- Match the opening sentences to the paragraphs of the passage.
- Discuss how you can tell where they belong.

Opening sentences

(a) Additives serve a range of purposes from colouring food to regulating its acidity.

(b) In Britain, people like their butter to be bright yellow.

(c) Both processing and storage can result in food losing its natural colour, so manufacturers re-create it – either to make food look more attractive or because consumers have come to expect foods to be in certain colours.

(d) Among the more widely used colours, tartrazine (E102) has been found to cause hyperactivity and other adverse reactions in a minority of consumers.

(e) In Britain, some 3750 substances may be legally added to the food you eat; nearly 3500 of these are flavourings, which need not be specified in anything other than general terms by the manufacturers who use them.

Paragraphs

1. Fewer than 10 per cent of all legal additives are synthetic, and natural and synthetic additives represent less than 0.5 per cent of all the food we eat. Medical experts place additives a long way down the list of food hazards, and so far only one person in about 1800 is known to have an adverse reaction to synthetic additives.

2. Some perform more than one function. For example, vitamin C (ascorbic acid) is used to prevent tinned fruit and fruit juice from turning brown, as well as to improve the baking quality of wheat, while citric acid is widely used as both a flavouring agent and an acidity regulator.

3. Without added colour, tinned peas, for example, would look an unappetising shade of olive green or grey. Critics argue that additives disguise the fact that processed foods are not really as nutritious as fresh produce; and that added flavours and colours create a taste for unnaturally strongly flavoured and brightly coloured foods.

4. This colour comes from beta carotene, which is found in grass and animal feed, and its intensity depends on the cow's ability to metabolise the compound into vitamin A. Jersey cattle, which do not efficiently metabolise beta carotene, produce much yellower butter than Friesians, which do. UK margarine and low-fat spread manufacturers enhance the appearance of their products – which would otherwise appear off-white – and cater for this British preference by adding yellow colouring. Although today's colouring agents are thought to be safe, several of the early coal-tar pigments – now no longer used – were potentially carcinogenic.

5. Some doctors claim that tartrazine and other nitrogen-based azo dyes – many of which have been banned in Britain – can affect some children's behaviour, making them ill-tempered and disobedient. Others point out that children with adverse reactions to these additives will often react to fruit or other natural foods which contain similar compounds.

Teachers' note Ask the pupils to work in pairs and give each pair a copy of this page. Explain that the text comes from a Reader's Digest report entitled *Foods that Harm, Foods that Heal*, and that the paragraphs of the text are in the correct order. The pupils should try different arrangements until they find the one that works best. Invite feedback, and discuss the way in which each paragraph supports its opening sentence – which expresses its main point (see page 7).

Developing Literacy
Sentence Level
Year 9
© A & C BLACK

Plan it

- Plan a paragraph of a discussion text about whether motorists should be made responsible for any accident involving a car and a bicycle.

> **!** Remember, you are planning only one paragraph and not the entire discussion.

Main point of paragraph
Cyclists are more likely to be injured than car drivers.

Ways of developing the main point

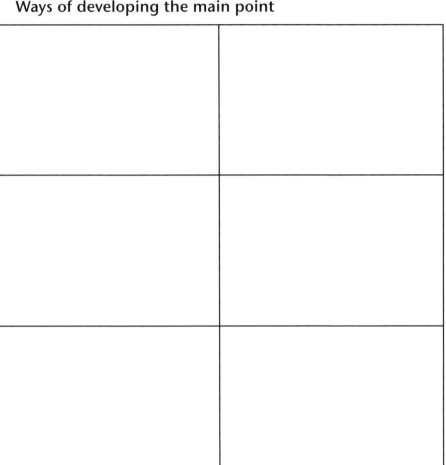

> Think of facts or opinions which support the main point.

> Consider how you will illustrate the facts or opinions.

> Make notes on the chart.

Useful connectives

- Now write your paragraph.

NOW TRY THIS!

- Think of an alternative way in which you could have developed the paragraph.
- Plan and write the new paragraph.
- Compare it with the first paragraph you wrote. Evaluate both paragraphs and suggest improvements.

Teachers' note Discuss the different ways in which the paragraph could be developed: for example, by writing about the dangers to cyclists; by evaluating the range of safety measures taken by motorists and cyclists; by including opinions collected from cyclists or motorists; by considering how accidents might happen and how cyclists and motorists are usually affected. See also page 7.

Developing Literacy
Sentence Level
Year 9
© A & C BLACK **29**

Opening words
STARTER

• What do you expect each paragraph to be about when you read the opening sentence?

① On occasions, the heavy stillness of the Twilight Woods is disturbed by violent storms which blow in from beyond the Edge.

Drawn there like moths to a flame, the storms circle the glowing sky – sometimes for days at a time. Some of the storms are special. The lightning bolts they release create stormphrax, a substance so valuable that – despite the awful dangers of the Twilight Woods – it acts like a magnet to those who would possess it.

② At its lower reaches, the Twilight Woods give way to the Mire.

It is a stinking, polluted place, rank with the slurry from the factories and foundries of Undertown which have pumped and dumped their waste so long that the land is dead. And yet – like everywhere else on the Edge – there are those who live here. Pink-eyed and bleached as white as their surroundings, they are the rummagers, the scavengers.

③ Those who manage to make their way across the Mire find themselves in a warren of ramshackle hovels and rundown slums which straddle the oozing Edgewater River.

This is Undertown. Its population is made up of all the strange peoples, creatures and tribes of the Edge crammed into its narrow alleys. It is dirty, over-crowded and often violent, yet Undertown is also the centre of all economic activity – both above-board and underhand.

④ It buzzes, it bustles, it bristles with energy.

Everyone who lives there has a particular trade, with its attendant league and clearly defined district. This leads to intrigue, plotting, bitter competition and perpetual disputes – district with district, league with league, tradesman with rival tradesman. The only matter which unites all leaguesmen is their shared fear and hatred of the sky pirates who dominate the skies above the Edge in their independent boats and prey off any hapless leaguesmen whose paths they cross.

From *Stormchaser* by Paul Stewart and Chris Riddell

Teachers' note Photocopy this page onto an OHT. Mask the OHT so that only the instruction and the first opening sentence are visible. Explain to the pupils that they should predict what the paragraph is going to be about and the *type* of detail which will be included (not what they think the places will be like). Reveal the rest of the paragraph and discuss whether or not it matches their predictions. Talk about how the opening sentence prepares the reader for the rest of the paragraph. Then repeat this for each of the three following paragraphs.

Developing Literacy
Sentence Level
Year 9
© A & C BLACK

Opening words

• Write the opening sentences for these paragraphs from the fairytale *The Emperor's New Clothes*.

①

He paid no attention to his soldiers, nor did he care about going out of the palace except to show off his clothes. He had a robe for every hour of the day, and if anyone were looking for him his servants would say, 'The emperor is in the wardrobe!'

②

Many visitors arrived every day. One day two rogues came. They passed themselves off as weavers and said that they knew how to weave the most exquisite cloth imaginable. Not only was the pattern amazingly beautiful but also the clothes made from the cloth had the special quality of being invisible to stupid people or people unfit for their jobs.

③

'Wearing them I could find out which people in my kingdom are stupid and not fit for their jobs; I can tell the wise ones from the stupid! Yes, that cloth must be woven for me at once!' And he gave the two rogues a huge sum of money in advance.

④

However, they had no thread at all on the looms. They demanded the best silk and the most magnificent gold thread. This they put in their bags and worked at the empty looms until far into the night.

⑤

But it made him feel a little uneasy to think that anyone who was stupid or unfit for his job couldn't see it. Of course he didn't believe that he himself needed to be afraid. Nonetheless he wanted to send someone else first to see how things stood. The whole city knew of the remarkable powers possessed by the cloth, and everyone was eager to see how stupid their neighbours were.

⑥

'He's the best one to see how the cloth looks, for he has brains and no one is better fitted for his job than he is!'

⑦

'Why, I can't see a thing!' But he didn't say so.

⑧

Then they pointed to the empty loom, and the poor old minister kept opening his eyes wider. But he couldn't see a thing, for there was nothing there.

Teachers' note The pupils should read the whole text before they begin writing the opening sentences. Ask them to identify the shifts in topic or the introduction of speech, and to deduce the type of information or ideas which are needed to begin the paragraph. Encourage them to use different ways of opening the paragraphs.

Developing Literacy
Sentence Level
Year 9
© A & C BLACK **31**

A new development

STARTER

- Choose one of these opening sentences for a paragraph.
- Develop the paragraph using words and phrases from the notepad.

Opening sentences for paragraphs

The amount of traffic in the city centre needs to be reduced because the roads are too narrow to cope with it.

A toll for entering the city centre would deter motorists who can find alternative routes.

Driving would be much easier for motorists whose visits to the city centre are essential.

A toll would be unfair on residents.

Students at the university would not be able to afford to pay the toll.

A toll-collecting point would slow down the traffic and cause queues.

An alternative would be to close the city centre to all traffic except for essential purposes such as loading, and for disabled drivers.

Words and phrases

Furthermore…
On the contrary…
In addition…
Apart from that…
Imagine that…
Not only… but also
Consider…
What is more…
On the other hand…
Moreover…

HONK!

Development

_____
_____
_____
_____
_____
_____
_____
_____
_____
_____
_____

Teachers' note Photocopy this page onto an OHT. Read the opening sentences with the class and ask the pupils to identify the text-type (an argument). Ask them to predict the purpose of each paragraph: for example, 'In this paragraph the writer is going to argue that a toll would reduce the amount of traffic in the city centre'. Allow the pupils a few minutes to discuss ideas for developing one of the paragraphs in groups. Invite one of the groups to write their paragraph on the OHT. Then wipe it clean and ask another group to write their development of a different paragraph.

Developing Literacy
Sentence Level
Year 9
© A & C BLACK

A new development

- Develop the following paragraph of an argument. The topic is whether supermarkets should import organic foods if the same items are being produced in the UK.

The information on the notepad will help. Choose the relevant information for your paragraph. Use **connectives** to link the ideas.

!

Many imported organic foods are cheaper than those grown in the UK.

Regulations for organic farming are more stringent in the UK than in many other countries.

In many countries labour is cheaper than in the UK.

Farm subsidies in some countries make it difficult for UK farmers to set competitive prices. Many UK suppliers are small.

Buyers from supermarkets say that they cannot buy enough for their needs.

Dealing with large suppliers makes it easier for supermarkets to control quality.

According to Ivor Bargin, managing director of Superbuy, most consumers shop with cost in mind. They want good food, but they want it cheap.

NOW TRY THIS!

- Use the information on the notepad to help you write another paragraph for the same argument.

Teachers' note Model the development of the paragraph by thinking aloud: for example, 'In this paragraph I shall argue that consumers want cheap food. That is the main point. I shall consider the effect this has on the buying policies of supermarkets. I could extend it by discussing ideals versus cost...'

Paragraph links
STARTER

• Underline the words and phrases which link each paragraph to the next.

I call it my talisman, my lucky token, and it always sits on the desk in front of me. It is my most treasured possession; and yet it is worth nothing at all – just an ordinary stone, about the size and shape of a pear. It was given to me some fifteen years ago by a parish priest on the Hebridean island of South Uist when I was a young reporter on a newspaper; and although I cannot now remember what the story I was covering was about, I have never forgotten the gift of the stone.

It had been found, so I was told, during the excavation of an archaeological site on South Uist near a tiny crofting village called Kilpheder, which stands on a long stretch of low-lying fertile grassland called *machair* in Gaelic – a carpet of rich, springy turf on top of sand-dunes. It was a very old site, and had been buried under the sand for many centuries. It turned out to be an ancient homestead of the type known as a 'wheel-house' because its design was just like that of a wheel: a round house with room-partitions like the spokes of a wheel radiating from a central hub. These houses were occupied by a people called the Picts about 1500 years ago – the Picts had been living in Scotland for many centuries before the 'Scots' as we know them today arrived and took over the country.

The stone I was given was found on the floor of one of the chambers of the wheel-house at Kilpheder. Both ends of the stone, the blunt end and the sharper end, showed signs of having been chipped; and on the surface of the stone were some irregular dark patches, like grease-marks. When I hold the stone in my hand, these grease-marks fit exactly the flesh-pads of my palm and fingers, because these dark marks, I was assured, had been made by sweat; they were the grimy sweat-marks of people who had used the stone as a primitive hammer all those long centuries ago.

To hold this stone in my own hand gave me then, and gives me still, a shiver of excitement. It works as a kind of time-machine which transports me suddenly and vividly into the intimate physical presence of the Pictish families who lived and died in that huddled, sunken house. These were not the wild and painted savages the Roman historians portrayed so patronisingly when the legions invaded Scotland; these were ordinary peaceful farmers who grazed their livestock on the *machair*, grew corn which they ground into flour for bread, caught fish – and used handy stones from the seashore as improvised hammers.

From *Introducing Archaeology* by Magnus Magnusson

Teachers' note Ask the pupils to work in pairs and give each pair a copy of this page. Read the opening sentence of the first paragraph and ask them what is unusual about it. Discuss the effect of the sentence and draw out the way in which it makes the reader want to read on. Focus on the use of pronouns and nouns to link one paragraph to the next: for example, *It had been found, The stone I was given, To hold this stone*.

Developing Literacy
Sentence Level
Year 9
© A & C BLACK

Paragraph links

- Think of an object which is special to you in some way and which has a story or idea you can write about.
- Write three paragraphs about the object and the story or ideas connected with it.

Use the passage about the lucky stone as a model.

!

Paragraph 1

Begin with the object. Use a pronoun so that you do not name the object at first.

Say why the object is important, but don't tell its whole story.

Sum up your feelings about the object.

Paragraph 2

Refer to the object again, using a pronoun. Tell its story, briefly (reveal the details gradually, over the three paragraphs).

Introduce the ideas connected with the object or widen the story to include other things.

Give more details about the object and the ideas or story linked with it.

Leave the reader with something to think about.

Paragraph 3

Refer to the object again, using a noun. Link this reference to the details revealed in the previous paragraph.

Give more details about the object's story.

End with a comment to sum up.

NOW TRY THIS!

- Re-read what you have written. Underline the words which link each paragraph to the ones before and after it.

Teachers' note The pupils will need to refer to the passage in the starter activity. Before the lesson, ask them to think about, or bring to school, an object which has meaningful associations. Encourage them to ask one another questions about their objects. When writing their paragraphs, they could use some of the words from the starter passage: for example, *I call it..., It always..., It is my...*

Pronoun purposes

STARTER

• Underline the ⟨pronouns⟩ in these sentences.

1. This is James. He is my brother.

2. I bought myself a present with my first month's salary.

3. Selima and I had heard that that film was good, so we went to see it for ourselves.

4. After growling and barking at one another as if declaring war, the two dogs settled down and, although they never became friends, war never broke out; they seemed to have accepted a truce.

5. Jones and Smith were the only ones who had been in the building when the money was stolen. Each accused the other of the theft.

6. That is their house; this one is mine.

7. I have heard that you have played for the city under-15 football team. Is that right?

8. I saw everything the woman did while she was there, but I could do nothing about it.

9. What did he say?

10. Which way did he go?

11. Whose is that van over there?

12. It belongs to the man who came to fix the roof.

13. Lauren and I entered the singing competition; each of us won a prize.

14. We heard about Alex and Sam's climbing accident. Everyone was pleased that they were both rescued and that neither of them was badly injured.

15. This is the car which was spotted in the car park yesterday.

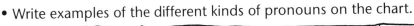

• Write examples of the different kinds of pronouns on the chart.

Pronouns used instead of nouns	Pronouns that help to separate or identify people or things	Pronouns that show possession
I, me, mine	each other	my
Pronouns that show relationships	**Demonstrative pronouns (used to 'point' to things)**	**Pronouns that ask questions**
who (for example, the girl who won the race)	this	What...?

Teachers' note Photocopy this page onto an OHT. Invite the pupils to come out and underline the pronouns, then ask them to contribute to the completion of the chart. This is an opportunity to revise personal, possessive and reflexive pronouns. Discuss what other purposes pronouns can have (see page 7 for notes on other types of pronouns and their purposes). Focus on the ways in which the pronouns are used to reveal or reinforce meaning in the sentences.

Developing Literacy
Sentence Level
Year 9
© A & C BLACK

Pronoun purposes

• Read the passages. Underline the **pronouns**.

What kind of man was Roget?

Peter Mark Roget (1779–1869) was one of those intellectual giants of the Victorian era who seemed to know everything about everything. The son of a Genevan pastor, he was brought up in London's French Protestant community and was sent to study medicine at Edinburgh University. He graduated as a doctor at the age of 19 and went on to become a founder of Manchester Medical School. But his interests were by no means confined to the medical sphere.

From 'The man who classified the English language' (*The Week*)

Football referee Melvin Sylvester knew there was only one penalty for fighting on the pitch. So when he lost his temper and threw a punch at one of the players, he sent himself off. Forty-two-year-old Mr Sylvester, a school caretaker and experienced referee, took over the running of the Andover and District Sunday League match between the Southampton Arms and Hurstbourne Tarrant British Legion in April 1998 when the appointed official was taken ill. All was going smoothly until Mr Sylvester, who also happened to be the manager of the Southampton Arms, reacted to what he claimed was a push by Hurstbourne player Richard Curd.

From *Great Sporting Mishaps* by Geoff Tibballs

• Write the pronouns on the chart to show how they are used.

Replacing nouns	Showing possession	Showing relationships	'Pointing' to things	Referring to things without specifying what they are

NOW TRY THIS!

• Read passages from other text-types and identify the pronouns.

• Draw and complete charts to show how the pronouns are used in each text.

• Compare how pronouns are used in different text-types.

Teachers' note The pupils are likely to find the personal, possessive and reflexive pronouns the easiest to identify. Encourage them to consider the ways in which these link parts of the paragraph and to look for pronouns of other kinds: for example, relative pronouns such as *who* and *which*, both of which can also be used as interrogative pronouns (see page 7).

Get connected

STARTER

- Read the passage. Underline the **connectives**.

FREED MAN TAKES OFF IN SOLICITOR'S CAR

By John Staples

Solicitor Douglas Wright was pleased to have got his client freed on bail – but less delighted when the man stole his BMW immediately after the court hearing.

The 30-year-old man was bailed at Kilmarnock Sheriff Court after appearing on a charge of being drunk in charge of a vehicle.

But when the defendant, who cannot be named for legal reasons, left the courtroom on Monday, he walked straight into the lawyers' room where he stole the keys to Mr Wright's BMW 5 series. He then jumped in the vehicle and drove off, leaving the lawyer stranded.

Later, an embarrassed Mr Wright relived the incident – and admitted he had been the butt of a few jokes by his colleagues.

When the solicitor noticed his keys were missing, he ran to the car park to find his W-reg BMW had gone.

Mr Wright, 58, who has handled cases at the court for nearly 30 years, called the police before looking on the building's CCTV footage. He could only see the back of a figure making its way into the lawyers' room but he thought it was his client. So he told the police the defendant's address and they found the man sitting in the £21,000 vehicle at a traffic light.

When police arrested him, the thief then asked if Mr Wright would represent him again. Mr Wright refused.

The day afterwards, the man appeared in court and pleaded guilty to stealing the car. He was remanded in custody and will be sentenced later this month.

Mr Wright said: "The problem that you have got to realise is that when you work in law you deal with criminals."

From The Scotsman

Teachers' note Photocopy this page onto an OHT. Ask the pupils to identify the text-type (a newspaper recount) and to say what type of connectives they would expect to find in this text-type and why. They should look for simple linking connectives (such as *and* and *also*), and connectives showing relationships of time, contrast and consequence. Prompt discussion with questions such as 'What ideas or facts are linked by each connective?' 'What relationship does the connective show?' 'What makes these connectives suitable for this text-type?'

Developing Literacy
Sentence Level
Year 9
© A & C BLACK

Get connected

• Read the passage. Underline the **connectives**.

The modern coal industry

During the early part of the 1990s the government's review of our energy requirements concluded that coal was not the fuel of the future. Since then the amount of coal mined and the number of collieries have been cut dramatically. Only the most efficient and profitable mines have remained open as these are the only ones which can produce coal cheaply enough to compete with foreign imports. A major factor in the government's decision was that the electricity-generating companies could not guarantee that they would use as much coal in the future.

Coal is perceived to be a dirty fuel. Smoke from chimney stacks leads to acid rain if not filtered properly, and filtering the smoke is expensive. In addition, large areas of land are needed next to the power station to store the coal. Alternative sources of power are now more readily available. At present gas-fired power stations are cleaner and cheaper, and can respond more quickly to the changes in demand for electricity.

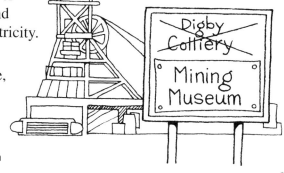

As a result many former coalmining areas have become zones of 'industrial blight': for example, in South Wales the only coal produced today comes from privately owned mines. There are no working mines owned by British Coal.

From *Letts Study Guide Geography* by Mike Clinch

• Complete the chart to show what relationships the connectives show, and what ideas or facts they link.

Type of connective	Examples	Ideas or facts linked by connective
Simple linking (for instance, *and*)		
Time (for instance, *then*)		
Cause and effect (for instance, *because*)		
Consequence (for instance, *so*)		
Reinforcing (for instance, *also*)		

NOW TRY THIS!

• Compare the types of connectives used in the passage above with those used in the recount about the stolen BMW.

• Discuss with a partner what makes the connectives appropriate for the text-type.

Teachers' note Before the pupils begin the activity, ask them to identify the text-type and to say how they can tell. Discuss what kind of connectives they expect to find in it. For the extension activity, the pupils will need to refer to the passage in the starter activity.

Locate the linkers

STARTER

- Read the passage. Underline the references back and the introductory words and phrases which connect the clauses, sentences and paragraphs.

A reference back is a connective word or phrase which refers to something already mentioned: for example, 'that day', 'the next time', 'the two of them'. An introductory word or phrase could be, or could act as, an adverb, conjunction, preposition or pronoun.

The church was so damp from the floods, that Master Ratsey had put a fire in the brazier which stood at the back, but was not commonly lighted till the winter had fairly begun. We boys sat as close to the brazier as we could, for the wet cold struck up from the flags, and besides that, we were so far from the clergyman, and so well screened by the oak backs, that we could bake an apple or roast a chestnut without much fear of being caught. But that morning there was something else to take off our thoughts; for before the service was well begun, we became aware of a strange noise under the church. The first time it came was just as Mr Glennie was finishing 'Dearly Beloved', and we heard it again before the second lesson. It was not a loud noise, but rather like that which a boat makes jostling against another at sea, only there was something deeper and more hollow about it. We boys looked at each other, for we knew what was under the church, and that the sound could only come from the Mohune Vault. No one at Moonfleet had ever seen the inside of that vault; but Ratsey was told by his father, who was clerk before him, that it underlay half the chancel, and that there were more than a score of Mohunes lying there. It had not been opened for over forty years, since Gerald Mohune, who burst a blood-vessel drinking at Weymouth races, was buried there; but there was a tale that one Sunday afternoon, many years back, there had come from the vault so horrible and unearthly a cry, that parson and people got up and fled from the church, and would not worship there for weeks afterwards.

We thought of these stories, and huddled up closer to the brazier, being frightened at the noise, and uncertain whether we should not turn tail and run from the church. For it was certain that something was moving in the Mohune vault, to which there was no entrance except by a ringed stone in the chancel floor, that had not been lifted for forty years.

However, we thought better of it, and did not budge, though I could see when standing up and looking over the tops of the seats that others beside ourselves were ill at ease; for Granny Tucker gave such starts when she heard the sounds, that twice her spectacles fell off her nose into her lap, and Master Ratsey seemed to be trying to mask the one noise by making another himself, whether by shuffling with his feet or by thumping down his prayer-book. But the thing that most surprised me was that even Elzevir Block, who cared, men said, for neither God nor Devil, looked unquiet, and gave a quick glance at Ratsey every time the sound came. So we sat till Mr Glennie was well on with the sermon.

From *Moonfleet* by J. Meade Falkner

Teachers' note Ask the pupils to work in pairs and give each pair a copy of this page. Read the passage with them and ask them to identify the text-type. Help them to identify the words and phrases used to link ideas in the passage, especially reference back: for example, *besides that* (see also page 8). Ensure that the pupils can recognise which of these are subordinating conjunctions introducing subordinate clauses (for example, *for, that* and *whether*).

Developing Literacy
Sentence Level
Year 9
© A & C BLACK

Locate the linkers

Some of the **connectives** have been removed from this passage.

- Fill the gaps with suitable connective words and phrases from the notepad.

Use each connective word or phrase only once.

!

Connective words and phrases

about	after	also	and so	and afterwards
as soon as	besides that	if	for	on the next day after
so	so that	that	though	what
when	which	while	yet	yet

So _____ we heard the sounds in church, being the Monday, _____ morning school was over, off I ran down street and across meadows to the churchyard, meaning to listen outside the church _____ the Mohunes were still moving. I say outside the church, for I knew Ratsey would not lend me the key to go in _____ what he had said _____ boys prying into things _____ did not concern them; and _____ , I do not know that I should care to have ventured inside alone, even if I had the key.

_____ I reached the church, not a little out of breath, I listened first on the side nearest the village, that is the north side; putting my ear against the wall, _____ lying down on the ground, _____ the grass was long and wet, _____ I might the better catch any sound that came. _____ I could hear nothing, _____ concluded that the Mohunes had come to rest again, _____ thought I would walk round the church and listen too on the south or sea side, for that their worships might have drifted over to that side, and be there rubbing shoulders with one another. _____ I went round, and was glad to get out of the cold shade into the sun on the south. But here was a surprise; _____ when I came round a great buttress _____ juts out from the wall, _____ should I see but two men, and these two were Ratsey and Elzevir Block. I came upon them unawares, and, lo and behold, there was Master Ratsey lying _____ on the ground with his ear to the wall, _____ Elzevir sat back against the inside of the buttress with a spy-glass in his hand, smoking and looking out to sea.

From *Moonfleet* by J. Meade Falkner

NOW TRY THIS!

- Look for connectives in texts you are studying. List the connectives which introduce subordinate clauses and refer back to ideas or information already mentioned.

Teachers' note Encourage the pupils to try different connective words and phrases in the gaps (in pencil) before writing their final choices. There is more than one possible solution. During the plenary session, discuss the type and purpose of the connectives in the passage.

A matter of fact
STARTER

- Read the passage.
- Underline examples in the passage of the features of information texts. Link them to the correct feature labels.

The insect body

An adult insect can be distinguished from other superficially similar creatures such as spiders and woodlice by its three main body regions – the head, thorax and abdomen – and its three pairs of legs. Most insects also have wings, which are not found in any of these other small animals. The head carries the mouthparts, which vary according to the diet, the eyes and a pair of antennae or feelers. The latter, varying from tiny bristles to large feather-like structures, are used for smelling and picking up tactile signals and sometimes for detecting sounds and heat.

The pronotum is a tough plate covering the front part of the thorax. It is often quite small, but in grasshoppers, beetles and many bugs it forms a conspicuous shield. There may also be a prominent rounded or triangular plate called the scutellum at the rear of the thorax. The wings, when present, are attached to the thorax. Most wings are membranous and supported on a network of veins; the spaces between the veins are known as cells. Beetles and some other insects have horny or leathery forewings, sometimes called elytra, which cover and protect the delicate hindwings. At rest these insects do not look as if they have wings at all.

The legs are also attached to the thorax. They vary in shape according to the habits of the insects, but generally have four main regions. The coxa is a short segment attaching the leg to the body. The femur is usually quite large and is followed by the tibia, which is usually the longest section of the leg. Beyond the tibia comes the tarsus or foot, which consists of up to five short segments and usually ends in a pair of claws. Crickets even have their ears on their front legs.

From *Collins Gem: Insects* by Michael Chinery

Features

| Setting the broad category |

| Narrowing it down to be more specific |

| Describing different aspects of the subject |

| Describing generic types |

| Verbs in the present tense |

| Connective words and phrases signalling distinctive categories of information |

| The third person |

| Technical vocabulary with some description |

Teachers' note Photocopy this page onto an OHT. First read the text and discuss how it is organised: it is introduced in a general way and then becomes more specific, describing the three sections of the insect's body in detail (see also page 8). The pupils could create a colour key, using a different colour OHT pen to colour each of the 'feature' boxes on the right, and underlining examples in the text in the appropriate colour.

Developing Literacy
Sentence Level
Year 9
© A & C BLACK

A matter of fact

- Use the notes to help you write another paragraph for the information text *The insect body*. This paragraph is about the abdomen.

- no limbs on abdomen
- many have pr of outgrowths (cerci) at rear: often hair-like – used as extra pair of antennae
- mayflies + silverfish → extra filament btwn cerci
- earwig cerci = sturdy pincers used in fights
- bush-crickets + some other insects – curved cerci grasp when mating
- many insects have prominent ovipostor (egg-layer) projecting from rear end

NOW TRY THIS!

- Use the format below to plan an information text about another type of living thing. Model its structure on the text *The insect body*.

| Set the broad category |
| Narrow it down to be more specific |
| Describe different aspects of the subject |
| Describe generic types |
| Return to the broad category to round off the text |

Teachers' note The pupils will need to refer to the completed starter activity. Before beginning the extension activity, point out that the starter passage is not complete; it should end with a paragraph which returns to the broad category to round off the text. Discuss how this can be done, with reference to other information texts.

Developing Literacy
Sentence Level
Year 9
© A & C BLACK **43**

What's the story?

STARTER

- To which text-type does this passage belong?

- Identify the distinctive features of this text-type. Write them in the boxes and link them to examples in the passage.

Features

Language style:

Person (main):

Person (other):

Tense:

Voice (main):

Voice (other):

Types of connectives:

Are quotations used?
Yes ☐   No ☐

Is punctuation:
simple? ☐
sophisticated? ☐

Are sentence structures:
simple? ☐
compound? ☐
complex? ☐

I didn't steal things as a child because I wanted them, I stole because it was a buzz and because I never really got caught. My parents might find out, but nothing happened to make me stop. They might make me take it back, like the time I stole money from a woman down the road a few weeks after we'd moved into the neighbourhood. She was outside with my big sister Shuna and I was in her kitchen. Her purse was on the table. I got such a rush from opening it, taking out the money, putting it in my pocket and closing the purse before she came in.

I hid the coins in my little camel skin handbag and I couldn't help jangling it around in front of Shuna as we walked home, asking her to guess how much I had in there. When she ignored me, I jangled it in front of my parents. They looked inside, of course, and demanded to know where I'd got it. I told them eventually, after exercising my imagination about fairies leaving it for me in the night, and they called the woman and said they were sending me over with it, on my own. I got to the gate and chickened out, leaving it under a stone. I ran home and lied. But nothing happened because we moved and I never saw the woman again.

At the age of five, I went to my third new school. The kids asked me where I was from. I didn't like this question because the answer I was given by my father wasn't quite right and the real answer was too complicated. I was born in Totnes; we lived in Dartmouth but then moved to Cornwall I think, and then to North Carolina in the States where my father was posted for two years on an exchange with the American Marines. Being a Royal Marine helicopter pilot, of which there are few, his knowledge was in great demand. We'd come back to Britain and lived again in Cornwall, then moved somewhere else in Cornwall, then to somewhere in Hampshire. My father said we were Scottish, but I'd never been there. That's what I told the kids: 'I'm from Scotland.' But by the time I'd worked out where I was from they were off on some other topic, asking me if I remembered something which had happened last year but then stopping with the words, 'Oh, but you weren't here larsh year.'

From *The Whole Story: A Walk Around the World*, by Ffyona Campbell

Teachers' note Ask the pupils to work in pairs and give each pair a copy of this page (different pairs could work on different features of the text). They could create a colour key, using a different colour pencil to colour each of the feature boxes on the right, and underlining examples in the text in the appropriate colour. Allow about ten minutes and then invite feedback about the stylistic features (see page 8).

Developing Literacy
Sentence Level
Year 9
© A & C BLACK

What's the story?

The notes below are based on a | biography |.
The quotations in the biography have been
changed into reported speech.

Use the first person
and **direct speech**.
Add **connectives**.

- Write two paragraphs in the form of an
  | autobiographical recount |.

Paul swaps trumpet for £15 Zenith guitar at Rushworth and Dreapers (music store in Liverpool). Trumpet 14th birthday gift from father. Plays trumpet (*The Man with the Golden Arm* and other popular tunes). Realises can't sing with trumpet in mouth. If aspirations in singing, need something like guitar. Asks dad if mind swap. No. So goes to town + swaps. Gets guitar, comes home. Can't work out how to play. Doesn't realise it's because left-handed. Realises guitar wrong way round when sees pic of Slim Whitman (also l-handed).

Guitar upside-down; can't move bridge + nut wh. holds strings in tension → thin top string now passes thru' notches intended for thick bottom string; rattles about. Paul carefully shaves matchstick to make little block to put under top string (the one most used) to stop it moving around.

NOW TRY THIS!
- Make notes for two or three paragraphs of a biography of someone famous.
- Write the paragraphs.

Remember the differences and similarities between biography and autobiography.

!

Teachers' note Discuss that the biographical notes are written in the third person and the present tense, with no connectives and no complete sentences. Remind them of the stylistic conventions of autobiographical recounts and ask what changes they will need to make and what kind of connectives they will use. Their notes from the starter activity will help.

Developing Literacy
Sentence Level
Year 9
© A & C BLACK **45**

Explain yourself!

STARTER

- To which text-type does this passage belong? _____
- Identify the distinctive features of this text-type. Write them in the boxes and link them to examples in the passage.

Clouds and rain

Clouds are made up of droplets of moisture so tiny that at least a million of them are needed to form a single raindrop. How do these droplets accumulate in the churning atmosphere and form rain, drizzle, snow or hail?

Air is constantly conveying water vapour to the Earth's surface, but its capacity to do so is limited and depends largely on temperature. The warmer the air, the more water vapour it can hold, though air can hold only so much vapour at a given temperature, and at a certain point it is said to be saturated. Then the vapour condenses into microscopic droplets, releasing heat which allows it to keep rising. Furthermore, because air is constantly on the move, it can either cool down or warm up, depending on the time and the place. When it cools enough, it causes the water vapour it contains to condense out.

In fact, water has trouble condensing into droplets in the air unless it has something to cling to. The tiny 'condensation nuclei' it uses – usually specks of sea salt, dust, sand or other airborne particles – are plentiful at the Earth's surface but can be in very short supply in the upper atmosphere. When air is perfectly clean, it can hold more water vapour than is theoretically possible. It is then said to be in a state of supersaturation.

Clouds are aggregations of condensed water vapour suspended in the atmosphere. Clouds assume a limited number of shapes wherever they form, and each type allows observers to predict the weather a few hours ahead.

From How Weather Works: Understanding the Elements by René Chaboud

Features

Language style: _____

Type of vocabulary: _____

Person: _____

Tense: _____

Voice (main): _____

Voice (other): _____

Type of nouns: _____

Types of connectives: _____

Are sentence structures mainly:

simple? ☐

compound? ☐

complex? ☐

Teachers' note Ask the pupils to work in pairs and give each pair a copy of this page (different pairs could work on different features of the text). They could create a colour key, using a different colour pencil to colour each of the feature boxes on the right, and underlining examples in the text in the appropriate colour. Allow about ten minutes and then invite feedback about the stylistic features (see page 8). Discuss the types of paragraph openings in the passage, including those which indicate contrast and comparison (*In fact...*) and elaboration (*Air is..., Clouds are...*).

Developing Literacy
Sentence Level
Year 9
© A & C BLACK

Explain yourself!

- Use the notes to help you write another paragraph for the explanation text *Clouds and rain*. This paragraph is about what causes precipitation.

Add connectives.

What causes precipitation?

- Most precipitation forms in clouds (temp –0 + mixture of ice crystals + minute frozen water droplets)

- Assumption: water always → ice at below freezing temps; in upper atmos, something surprising: water can remain liquid even –0

- Such supercooled water droplets v unstable → freeze into tiny ice crystals spontaneously when contact solid. → Must go thru series of stages to grow: transfer (ice cryst grow up to ×10, while water droplets evap), growing cryst get heavy → start to fall, keep growing. Supercooled water droplets collide with them + freeze ('riming'), ice builds up on them → heavier → fall faster → come together → form snowflakes

NOW TRY THIS!

- Plan a short explanation text about another aspect of weather. Model its structure on the text *Clouds and rain*.

| First introduce the topic. Perhaps ask a question. | Develop the topic by focusing on why and how the process happens. | Summarise what has been explained. |

Teachers' note Before beginning, read the notes with the pupils. Ask them to consider which tense, person and type of sentence structure they will use in their writing. Remind them of connective words and phrases which indicate sequence and cause and effect (for example, *as a result, because of this, eventually, finally, next, so, then, this means that*).

Step by step
STARTER

- To which text-type does this passage belong? _____
- Identify the distinctive features of this text-type. Write them in the boxes and link them to examples in the passage.

Planning your Web site

You will be using a template in Microsoft Word to create your home page. You need to know what this will look like, as it will influence your planning. Therefore, we are going to open Microsoft Word, open a new document using the Personal Web Page template and take a sneak preview of the possibilities.

To open Microsoft Word: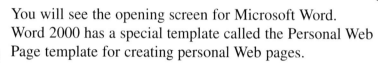

- ► Click on the Start menu button.
- ► Click on Programs.
- ► Click on the Microsoft Word icon.

You will see the opening screen for Microsoft Word. Word 2000 has a special template called the Personal Web Page template for creating personal Web pages.

To start a new Web page using this template:

- ► From the File menu select New.
- ► Click on the Web Pages tab and select Personal Web Page.

A home page will be automatically created for you, and it is ready for you to edit with your own personal information. At the top of the page there is a Contents list, showing all the sections in the document.

- ► Scroll down and find the sections on Biographical Information and Personal Interests.
- ► Scroll back up to the top of the page to the Contents list.
- ► Click on the Personal Interests bookmark to be taken automatically to the Personal Interests section of the page.
- ► Click the Back to Top bookmark to return to the top of the page.

Now you are ready to use your home page.

From Basic Web Page Creation using Word 2000 by A. A. Richards

Features

Language style:
_____

Type of vocabulary:
_____

Main verb mood:
_____

Tense:
_____

Is punctuation:
simple? ☐
sophisticated? ☐

Are sentence structures mainly:
simple? ☐
compound? ☐
complex? ☐

'Signposts' to help the reader follow the text

A signal for the end of the process

A closing statement to help the reader evaluate what has been done

---

Teachers' note Ask the pupils to work in pairs and give each pair a copy of this page (different pairs could work on different features of the text). They could create a colour key, using a different colour pencil to colour each of the feature boxes on the right, and underlining examples in the text in the appropriate colour. Allow about ten minutes and then invite feedback about the stylistic features (see page 8).

Developing Literacy
Sentence Level
Year 9
© A & C BLACK

Step by step

- Read the passage about sending an email.
- Rewrite the text in the form of instructions.

I sent an email

First I clicked on the Outlook Express icon. The Outlook Express screen appeared. On top of it was a dialogue box which said 'You are currently working offline. Would you like to go online now?' I clicked the 'No' box. I clicked the Create Mail icon and the New Message screen appeared. At the top it said 'To', 'Cc' and 'Subject'. I moved the cursor to 'To' and keyed in Roop's email address. I moved the cursor to 'Cc' (carbon copy) and keyed in Jenny's email address because I wanted to send the same message to her. I moved the cursor to 'Subject' and keyed in 'Ten pin bowling'. I clicked on the main message box (the large white area) and wrote my message. I went online. To do this, I clicked the File menu and scrolled down until I came to Working offline (which had a tick); I clicked Working offline so that the tick disappeared and it changed to Working online. I clicked the Send icon at the top of the screen. A dialogue box appeared saying 'Dial-up connection'; I clicked 'Connect'. Another dialogue box appeared, which said 'Sending your message'. The message was sent.

Heading _____

Instructions _____

Ending _____

Teachers' note The pupils should use the notes they made in the starter activity as a guide. Discuss that instruction texts can be either formal or informal, depending on the audience for whom they are intended. Encourage the pupils to use a similar style to that of the passage in the starter activity.

Developing Literacy
Sentence Level
Year 9
© A & C BLACK **49**

Adapted

STARTER

- To which text-type does this passage belong?

_____

- What are the usual stylistic and grammatical conventions of this text-type? How has the writer adapted these conventions?

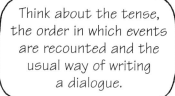

Think about the tense, the order in which events are recounted and the usual way of writing a dialogue.

Tag. The little kids' game, plain ordinary old tag, that's what he had us playing. Even though none of us was younger than eleven, and the older ones were big as men. Gil Warmun even had a triangle of beard on his chin. Warmun was 'it' for now, the tagger, chasing us; suddenly he swung round at me before I could dodge, and hit me on the shoulder.

'Nat!'

'Nat's it!'

'Go, go, go!'

Run round the big echoing space, trainers squealing on the shiny floor; try to catch someone, anyone, any of the bodies twisting and diving out of my way. I paused in the middle, all of them dancing round me ready to dodge, breathless, laughing.

'Go, Nat! Keep it moving, don't let it drop! Tag, tag!'

That huge voice was ringing out from the end of the room, Arby's voice, clear and deep, like a blow on a big gong. You did whatever that voice said, _now_; you moved quick as lightning. For the Company of Boys, Arby was director, actor, teacher, bossman. I dashed across the room towards a swirling group of them, saw the carrotty red head of little Eric Sawyer from Maine, chased him in and out and finally tagged him when he cannoned into a slower boy.

'Go, Eric, go – keep the energy up – '

The voice again, as Eric's scrawny legs scurried desperately through the noisy crowd – then suddenly a change, abrupt, commanding.

'_O-kay!_ Stop! That's it! Now we're going to turn that energy inside, inside us – get in groups of five, all of you, anywhere in the room. I want small boys with small, bigger guys together, each group matching.'

From _King of Shadows_ by Susan Cooper

Teachers' note Photocopy this page onto an OHT. The pupils should first complete the activity on pages 44–45. It will be helpful if they have a completed copy of page 44 for reference. Read the passage with the whole class, then ask the pupils to consider in turn each of the distinctive features of recounts and to say how this passage uses or adapts them. Discuss why they think the writer does this, and the effect of these adaptations.

Developing Literacy
Sentence Level
Year 9
© A & C BLACK

Adapted

- Rewrite the passage about playing tag. Change it so that it conforms with the usual stylistic conventions of recounts. Use conventional grammar for sentences and dialogue.

Write complete sentences.

Write in the past tense, recounting events in the order in which they happened.

Introduce or end speech with words to show who is speaking.

We were playing tag; the little kids' game, plain ordinary old tag. That's what he had us playing.

- Compare your changed version of the passage with the original. Describe the different effects.
- Why do you think the writer chose to adapt the conventions?

Teachers' note Ask the pupils to work in pairs. For the extension activity, encourage them to take turns to read aloud sections of the rewritten text and the corresponding part of the original, and to notice the different effects. During the plenary session, discuss the effects of the grammatical adaptations.

Language challenge

STARTER

• Identify the text-types. Comment on the style of language used:

> formal or informal?

> personal or impersonal?

> direct or indirect?

> simple or sophisticated?

1 My father and I walked on by the horses while our passengers on the front of the wagon laughed and talked, and one of them started singing a coarse song, but stopped when my father objected. Then for some reason I fell a bit behind the wagon, and as I did so I noticed the parcel the men had put on the back showing out in the strong moonlight. It was a bulky, long, shapeless sort of bundle contained in a big sack, and it wobbled in a fashion that made it seem, to my boyish eyes, as though it had something alive in it. This roused my curiosity, though at the same time it gave me a creepy kind of feeling.

From *Seventy Years a Showman* by 'Lord' George Sanger

2 Ignoring your human by withdrawing your attention is a powerful training tool. Simply turn your back firmly away from the erring human, giving no eye contact, and sit quietly thinking of higher things.

From *One Hundred Ways for a Cat to Train its Human* by Celia Haddon

4

Daily Detritus, 9 August 2002

Keep swill off doorsteps
By Ivor Porker

Residents of Much Fussing are up in arms about the pigswill processing plant to be opened shortly to the east of the village.

"The smell will make life here very unpleasant," said Rhona Mile, 43. "It should not be built so near to people's homes."

A spokesperson from Trotters, the company building the plant, said that their ultra-modern processes would mean that there would be no smell whatsoever, and that people should check the facts before protesting.

3 The Border Collie, named after the border between Scotland and England, has a strong eye, which enables it to hold a sheep with its menacing stare until the sheep either stands still or moves backwards. It is expected to run between 64 and 80 km a day, herding sheep, a task which calls for great stamina.

Size: Height 46–54 cm, weight 14–22 kg.

Lifespan: 12–14 years.

Identifying features: Coat can be rough or smooth in a variety of colours, although white markings should not be too pronounced.

Character: High-powered, intelligent working dog.

Pet suitability: Not a good domestic pet. Demands careful handling and plenty of freedom to roam.

Based on *Collins Gem: Dogs* by Wendy Boorer

Teachers' note The pupils should first complete the activities on pages 42–51. Split the class into small groups and give each group a copy of this page. First discuss how to identify the different language styles. Remind the pupils that direct language is usually in the first person and, if the reader is addressed, uses *you*; indirect language is usually in the third person, even when addressing the reader (for example, *readers could try this*). Ask each group to work on a different passage, considering verb form, person, tense, voice, sentence structure, punctuation and dialogue.

Developing Literacy
Sentence Level
Year 9
© A & C BLACK

Language challenge

- For each passage in the starter activity, identify the stylistic conventions of the language used. Complete the chart.

Write examples from the passages on the chart.

Style of language

Passage and text-type	Formal or informal?	Personal or impersonal?	Direct or indirect?	Simple or sophisticated?
1				
2				
3				
4				

- Choose one passage to rewrite in a different style (for example, changing the language from formal to informal).

First make notes about the types of changes you will make.

NOW TRY THIS!

Teachers' note The pupils should first complete the activities on pages 42–51. They will need to refer to copies of the starter activity. Ask pupils who complete the extension activity to consider whether their rewritten passage sounds 'right', and to explain their answer.

Developing Literacy
Sentence Level
Year 9
© A & C BLACK

Setting the standard
STARTER

- Match the labels to the passages. Label each passage with the correct letter.
- Explain your answers.

I heard the pools closing nxt wk B/C of drty chngng rms. PCB if U no NEthg. CU L8R BBFN.

1

Hi! How are things? I just come back from the pool an'… you should see the state of it… real filthy… Them cleaners should be sacked, shouldn't they?

2

I was appalled at the condition of the changing rooms last week. Their dirty condition poses a serious threat to the health of users.

3

Guess what? My mum's written to the manager of the leisure centre to complain about the dirty pool! About time someone did. Maybe it'll be OK by the summer holidays.

4

Yes, I think so too. They should get it cleaned up. You feel like you'll catch something there.

5

There should be stiffer penalties imposed on the proprietors of public amenities which are found to be deficient in some way. Responsibility. That is what they owe the public – the people who pay their salaries.

6

Labels

A	An email to a friend
C	A letter to a company
E	A text message to a friend

B	A speech
D	A phone call to a friend
F	A postcard to a friend

Teachers' note Photocopy this page onto an OHT. Invite the pupils to read the passages aloud before they match the labels to them. Draw out aspects of standard and non-standard English as well as the level of formality of the passages. Discuss the contexts in which standard and non-standard English are appropriate, and which forms of English the pupils would use when speaking or writing for different audiences.

Developing Literacy
Sentence Level
Year 9
© A & C BLACK

54

Setting the standard

The words of the speakers have been rewritten in standard English.

- Write in the speech bubbles the words the people might have spoken. Use non-standard English.

> Use slang expressions and dialect. **!**

> There is a good chance that it might rain.

Fair looks like it'll pour down.

> Those two dogs fought ferociously until they were separated by their owners.

> Nobody saw anything suspicious happening in the alley this afternoon. This is very surprising, since a great many people are known to have been there.

> It was exceptionally quiet in the house while we were working on our computer.

> We had a very enjoyable day. I was delighted to catch a large fish which we ate for supper.

> I would like chips and a bread roll, please. Would you mind not putting any salt on the chips?

NOW TRY THIS!

- Re-read what you have written. Notice the differences between standard and non-standard English.
- Make a chart to show the types of difference, with examples.

Type of difference	Standard English example	Non-standard English example
Non-agreement of pronouns and nouns	those dogs	them dogs

Teachers' note Encourage the pupils to think of dialect (from any region) and slang expressions to replace parts of the sentences on the cards. It may be useful to discuss and list features of non-standard English (such as those in the thought bubbles on page 57).

Write standard English

STARTER

- Read the girl's story.
- Underline the examples of non-standard English.
- Suggest standard English alternatives.

Some of the words are from the dialect of Northeast England. The glossary will help.

Mike an' Joan's weddin' wur a disaster from the word go, man. It began wi' claggy weather an' a thunner pash. We wuz all hangin' around at the kirk, wonderin' wur the best man was. One of the bairns giv 'im a ring on 'is mobile. He'd slept in. We'd warned 'im he'd get wrong if 'e did that. 'E can never get up on time, but he'd got a canny new alarm clock – an' then set it wrong.

Then the priest tuk sick an' cudden' come. The stand-in priest wur an hour late becuz 'e missed the boos, like.

There we were all trig in our best cloots, wi' no bride an' groom either. It turns out the weddin' cars wuz late, too. What else could go wrong?

Nowt else went wrong during the service, an' the reception went well – except that the honeymoon suite wur double-booked. 'We're gannin' hame,' says Mike an' Joan an' off they went, 'er in 'er weddin' dress, like, walkin'.

Glossary

bairns	children
canny	good, excellent, fine
claggy	sticky
cloots	clothes
gannin'	going (*gan* = go)
get wrong	be rebuked
kirk	church
nowt	nothing
thunner pash	thunderstorm
trig	neat, smartly dressed

Teachers' note Photocopy this page onto an OHT. Read the girl's story aloud and invite the pupils to identify examples of non-standard English. Discuss that spoken English often makes use of 'fillers' such as *man* and *like*. Talk about why the language style of the story is appropriate in the context of a girl talking to her friend; also discuss the problems someone from another region might have when listening to her.

Developing Literacy
Sentence Level
Year 9
© A & C BLACK

56

Write standard English

You need a tape recorder.

- Work with a partner. Tell your partner a brief story of an experience of your own (it could be a wedding or any other important occasion on which something funny or unusual happened). Record one another's stories.

- Transcribe your story.

- Underline any non-standard English you used. Look for:

dialect words

slang words

adjectives used as adverbs

non-agreement of subject and verb

them or they used instead of those; what used instead of which or who, and so on

inconsistency of tenses

double negatives

NOW TRY THIS!

- Rewrite your recount as a short story to be published.

Use standard English. Think about the audience and purpose.

!

Teachers' note The pupils will need access to tape recorders or other sound-recording devices. If computers with voice-recognition software are available, the pupils could edit their stories on screen and rewrite them for the extension.

Small talk

STARTER

Some friends have just returned to school after the holidays.

• Read this transcript of their conversation.

Sarah: Been on holiday then?

Gemma: Yeah – Florida for two weeks and London for a weekend.

Sarah: Lucky thing. Did ya go to Disney World?

Gemma: Yeah, it was great. Thought it would just be for kids, but it's cool… Hi, Mark.

Mark: Hi Gem. Hi Sarah. You two swapped all the gossip already?

Sarah: Cheek. We were talkin' 'bout holidays as it happens. You bin anywhere nice?

Mark: Yeah. I went to the Lakes for a week. Me sister was a right pain the whole time though. Did me head in. What about you two?

Sarah: Me, I went for a walk t' the end of the road, but Gem's flown half-way round the world.

Gemma: It seems ages ago. If only… hey, Milly. MILL! Cool shoes. Let's have a look.

Milly: Thanks, Gem. Hi Sarah, Mark. D'you know whose class we're in this term?

Sarah: Love the colour.

Mark: Dunno. I'll ask Tim. He'll know. Knows everything before the rest of the world. TIM!

Tim: Alright mate?

Mark: Whose class we in?

Tim: Mrs Murray's.

Milly: Nice one! She's pretty cool.

Sarah: I'm just off… See ya up there, yeah?

Mark: How come you always know everything before the rest of us?

Tim: It's hardly breaking news! It's been on the board for about an hour. Y'know, the big square thing in the basement?

Gemma: Yeah yeah, but we don't need to read notices with you around to do it for us! Hey, it's nine o'clock. Time to make a move. Let's go and bag a table.

Teachers' note Give each pupil a copy of this page. Allocate parts to the pupils and ask them to read the passage aloud. Then invite different pupils to re-read some of the lines and discuss how the spoken form can vary according to who reads it. Ask the pupils to consider what is lost in the written form: for example, intonation and expression, body language and eye contact, spontaneity, and response to other speakers and the context. Discuss other differences between spoken and written language.

Developing Literacy
Sentence Level
Year 9
© A & C BLACK

Small talk

- Use the conversation to help you identify the differences between spoken and written language. Find examples in the passage and write them on the chart.

You will find many of the features listed, but not all of them. **!**

Feature of spoken language	Examples
Informal vocabulary (for example, *got* rather than *received*)	
Slang or dialect words	
Non-standard grammatical structures	
Fillers (for example, *er, um*)	
'Tag' questions (for example, *Isn't it?*, *Don't they?*)	
'Sentences' which are not really sentences (for example, *No way!*, *The best!*)	
Social language (for example, *Nice day!*) which creates relationships between speakers rather than communicating meaning	
Interruptions	
Revision of meaning (beginning to say something and then changing part way through)	
Incomplete sentences which are 'left hanging'	
Response to the audience and the context	
Communicating meaning in the fewest possible words	
Repetition	
Hesitation (sentences begun, stopped and then re-started)	

NOW TRY THIS!

- Listen to people talking and notice how their speech differs from written language. Record your observations on another copy of the chart above.

Teachers' note The pupils will need to refer to the passage in the starter activity. During the plenary session, draw out the differences between everyday spoken language and written language: for example, when speaking informally we often leave sentences unfinished, add 'tag' questions, and so on. The extension can be done for homework (the pupils will need another copy of the chart).

Sign of the times
STARTER

- Read these quotations from the *Daily Mirror*, 29 November 1919.
- How can you tell from the language (rather than the subject-matter) that they are from an old newspaper?

From the politics column

I hear that the Government have taken an interesting step to control the expenditure of public departments. Hitherto it has been the practice of Ministers in promoting public Bills connected with their respective Departments to move the requisite financial resolution.

From the fashion column

Instead of the small toques formerly fashionable at afternoon dances I see that the new crownless turban is being much worn. The hair is revealed, of course, and the effect is very much of an ornate hair ornament.

Advertisement

Unruly hair is effectively controlled with Pears' Solidified brilliantine. It imparts life and gloss yet it is not oily; is clean, easy to apply, and its fresh, unobtrusive perfume is as attractive as its compact and handy form.

From the gossip column

I have just seen the newest in men's collars from Germany. They are made of thin wood and are really quite comfortable. They are being sold on the streets to our men at Cologne at four a penny, and look, an officer friend tells me, quite jolly with khaki.

From the children's section

My dear boys and girls, – owing to our small space I shall only be able to give you the usual Painting Competition to-day. Rather an exciting picture, isn't it? I am sure you are all very fond of Silver Fox – he is such a plucky chap.

Your affectionate Uncle Dick

From the fashion column

It is absolutely it to wear a dainty little cap of the Juliet variety (and black for choice) at theatre or dances, while two of last week's brides chose Dutch caps in white or gold lace with clusters of berries to further enhance their pretty bridesmaids. The point over each ear, which is slightly wired, is so becoming, you know.

From the sports page

This is the last day of the great *Daily Mirror* competition which entitles twenty of our readers to twenty-five guinea seats when Georges Carpentier meets Joe Beckett for the championship of Europe at the Holborn Stadium on December 4.

The letters have been of such extraordinary merit that they have been extremely difficult to judge. Every section of the public appears to have been interested in the competition.

Teachers' note Photocopy this page onto an OHT. Read the quotations with the class and encourage the pupils to look for aspects of language, rather than of context, which indicate the era when the newspaper was published: these include sentence structure, vocabulary, punctuation and use of clichés.

Developing Literacy
Sentence Level
Year 9
© A & C BLACK

60

Sign of the times

- Look through a recent newspaper or magazine.
- Record on the chart anything a reader from 1919 would find either incorrect or difficult to understand.

Language or grammar feature	Examples
New nouns	*nimby, nimbyism*
New verbs	*televise*
New informal or slang expressions	*cool, wicked*
Modern sentence structures and expressions	*Get a life!*
Modern punctuation	*Omitted apostrophes: Woolworths, Boots*

NOW TRY THIS!

- Rewrite the quotations from the *Daily Mirror* in a modern style.
- Make notes to explain the changes you have made.

Teachers' note Provide a selection of recent newspapers and magazines. The pupils will also need to refer to copies of the starter activity. This could be linked with word-level work on word-formations (for example, acronyms, such as *quango*); words formed by analogy, such as *telethon* (from *television* and *marathon*); and blends, such as *biodegradable* (from *biology* and *degradable*).

Foreign affairs
STARTER

Many |synonyms| in English originally came from French and Latin: for example, *happiness* (from Old English) has the synonyms *joy* (from French) and *felicity* (from Latin).

- Find synonyms to fill the gaps on the chart.
- Fill in the empty rows with synonyms of your own.

Old English	French	Latin
rise	mount	
ask		interrogate
fast	firm	
kingly		regal
holy		consecrated
	flame	conflagration
twist		revolve
gum		adhere
silly		
buy		
	centre	
call, yell		
boldness		
	aged	
heavy	massive	
	criminal	reprobate
	fury	ire
end		
	commence	

Teachers' note Photocopy this page onto an OHT. The pupils will need access to thesauruses and etymological dictionaries. Mask the chart and reveal one row at a time; the pupils could 'race' to find words to fill the gaps. Encourage them to guess first, then to use a thesaurus if necessary, and finally to check the derivation of the word. Afterwards, discuss how they could guess the derivations without looking them up, by using known foreign words such as *commencer* (French) and *nucleus* (Latin).

Developing Literacy
Sentence Level
Year 9
© A & C BLACK

Foreign affairs

Investigate ways in which English has changed over time

- Write **synonyms** for the words below.
- From which language do you think each synonym comes?

Try to work out which language the synonyms come from before you look them up.

!

Word	Synonyms	Source languages
big	*gigantic*	*Greek*
bright		
broad		
glue		
hill		
small		
strange		

NOW TRY THIS!

- Choose a piece of your own written work.
- Find synonyms for some of the words you used. Investigate the sources of the synonyms.

Teachers' note Ask the pupils to work in small groups. They should brainstorm synonyms for the words and try to work out the language of origin before looking them up. To help with the derivations, encourage them to think of words they have come across from other languages which have similar components.

Glossary

active (of a verb) A verb whose subject does the action: for example, *they shouted.*

adjective A word that describes a noun: for example, *blue, round, tall.*

adverb A word that gives information about a verb: for example, *she shouted loudly.*

agent The agent of a verb does the action: for example, *the boy kicked the ball; the ball was kicked by the boy* (the boy is the agent).

autobiographical recount A recount in the first person in which someone writes about his or her experiences.

auxiliary verb One of a small group of verbs which combine with a main verb to form tenses: for example, *they were watching; we should have known.*

biography The story of a person's life, written by someone else.

clause A section of a sentence which contains a verb: for example, *I laughed; she painted a picture.*

complex sentence A sentence which has at least one main clause and one or more subordinate clauses: for instance, *The woman ran ahead, singing as she went, while the others walked behind.*

compound sentence A sentence consisting of two or more main clauses joined by a conjunction: for instance, *I like swimming but Jane prefers running.*

conjunction A 'joining' or 'link' word: for example, *and, while, although.*

connective A word or phrase used to link words, phrases, clauses, sentences or paragraphs: for example, *I like swimming but Jane prefers running; we go there whenever we can.*

continuous tense A tense of a verb, formed with the participle *-ing* and one or more auxiliary verbs, which implies an ongoing action: for instance, *I was singing; we shall be singing.*

demonstrative pronoun A pronoun used to point to things: for example, *Look at that; What are these?*

determiner A word that introduces a noun phrase: for example, *a, any, each, my, seven, that.*

direct speech Spoken words placed between quotation marks (speech marks).

finite verb A verb that has a tense and a subject: for example, *I was looking; they had seen it.*

imperative The command form of a verb: for example, *go, mix, take.*

indirect speech Speech that reports the substance of what was said, without the use of quotation marks.

main clause A clause that can stand alone as a sentence and contains a finite verb: for example, *the forest consists mainly of pine trees.*

modal verb A type of auxiliary verb that helps the main verb to express different meanings: for example, *can, must, ought.*

non-finite verb A verb that has no tense or subject: for example, *to fit, fitting.*

noun A word that names a person, place or thing: for example, *a river, the Thames, a tributary.*

noun phrase A phrase which acts as a noun: for example, *the green bus, a certain book.*

object The object of an active verb has the action done to it: for instance, *the girl kicked the ball.*

passive (of a verb) A verb whose subject has the action done to it: for example, *the ball was kicked by the girl; the money was stolen.*

person (of a verb) This can be singular or plural: for example, *I go, we go* (first person); *you go* (second person); *she goes, they go* (third person).

personal pronoun A pronoun that represents a person or thing: *I, you, he, she, it, we, you, they.*

phrase A group of words that does not contain a verb: for instance, *along the road, for a while.*

possessive pronoun A pronoun that indicates ownership: for example, *my/mine, your/yours.*

preposition A word that shows a relationship between things, people or ideas in a sentence: for example, *along, by, from, with.*

pronoun A word used instead of a noun: for example, *he, them, it.*

reference back A connective word or phrase which refers to something already mentioned: for example, *that evening, both of us, since then.*

relative pronoun A pronoun that links places, people or things in a sentence: for example, *that, which, who, whom, whose.*

sentence A group of words that makes complete grammatical sense, ending in a full stop, question mark or exclamation mark.

simple sentence A sentence that has only one main verb (and therefore only one clause): for instance, *The woman crossed the road.*

simple tense A tense of a verb, formed without the participle *-ing*, which suggests something that is, was or will be done; is habitual; or is true at all times: for instance, *he will buy it tomorrow; she catches the number 12 bus; I live in Wales.*

subordinate clause A clause that makes sense only with another (main) clause: for instance, *she looked at the flower as if it could speak to her.*

synonyms Words with the same or similar meanings: for example, *joy, happiness, delight.*

tense The form of a verb that indicates time (past, present or future).

topic sentence A sentence in a paragraph which says what the paragraph is about.

verb A word or group of words that indicates action or a state of being: for example, *is, grew.*

Developing Literacy: Sentence Level Year 9 © A & C BLACK